THE FIX
for *cravings*

THE FIX
for *cravings*

One(s) that didn't work, and now one which WORKS

CYNTHIA MYERS-MORRISON, EdD
DAVE AVRAM WOLFE, MS, RD

ISBN: Hardcover   978-1-7960-9166-3
               Softcover   978-1-7960-9165-6
               eBook   978-1-7960-9164-9

Print information available on the last page.

Rev. date: 03/05/2020

To order additional copies of this book, contact:
Xlibris
1-888-795-4274
www.Xlibris.com
Orders@Xlibris.com
763294

CONTENTS

DEDICATIONS

Dave Avram Wolfe MD, RD

To my mentor Bitten Jonsson for her time, energy and
dedication to our shared passion; to my mother, Judy,
for showing me what recovery looks like; and to my
wife Kelly for showing endless patience and love

Cynthia Myers-Morrison, EdD

To Judy Wolfe and Kate for their untiring support

To Cassandra who died too early

To Candace who lives and loves

To Norma who birthed me when she had two woodburning
stoves (to cook and heat the quonset hut) and in 97 years
of life saw my father Robert fly off to WWII, Korea, and
Viet Nam, saw the Minuteman Missles go into the ground
and come out, and giggled over bridge hands and geneaolgy
finds. My father died too early. Just ask my mother!

To Peter Morrison for loving me and inviting me to love him

And to all those who may benefit from THE FIX for cravings

Do you desire the following:

FREEDOM from CRAVINGS and other OBSESSIONS

NEED FOR DEFINED ABSTINENCE (not just from food!)

FREEDOM TO BE AND BECOME

FREEDOOM from FOOD ADDICTION
and OTHER ADDICTIONS

https://lightofcindy.wordpress.com/ and https://www.triggerfreenutrition.com
THEFIXforcravings@gmail.com and David@triggerfreenutrition.com

DISCLAIMERS

This book is only intended as a reference volume, not as a medical manual. The information provided here is designed to help you make informed decisions about your health (physical, emotional and/or medical.) It is not intended as a substitute for any type of treatment you may have been prescribed by your clinician or doctor. If you suspect you have a medical problem, we urge you to seek competent medical help immediately. If you choose to use any of the material from this book for yourself or anyone else, the authors and publisher assume no responsibility for your actions and the results of your actions.

Although I am a registered dietitian, I am not a physician. I cannot diagnose, prescribe, and/or treat disease states whether physical, emotional or medical. Some of the nutrition advice provided is not universally accepted as evidence-based practice. It is not sponsored, approved, recommended or endorsed by the following: United States Department of Agriculture (USDA), FDA (Food and Drug Administration), NIH (National Institutes of Health), American Heart Association (AHA), American Diabetes Association (ADA), or Academy of Nutrition and Dietetics (AND). Always consult with your physician/medical provider prior to adopting a food plan or making dietary changes. If you choose to use any of the material from this book for yourself or anyone else, the authors and publisher assume no responsibility for your actions. Dave Avram Wolfe

A NOTE FROM AN AUTHOR (CYNTHIA)

Dear Reader,

- If you are interested in finding ways to support your health and well-being, this book is for you.
- If you have a problem with eating compulsively or have food addictions or food allergies or other disordered eating, this book is for you.
- If you want clarity of mind and freedom from brain fog, this book is for you.
- If you have aching joints and feet, this may be a book for you.
- If you are suffering from X (fill in the blank), this may be a book for you.

This is the book I wish someone had given to me in 1971 when I knew I had a problem with *thinking about food* and did not yet know I had a problem with alcohol, drugs, sex, workaholism, caretaking, over-responsibility, under-responsibility, love, acquisition, cigarettes, clutter, artificial sweeteners, diet sodas, migraines, sugar, grain, and other food allergies. 202 1b

In 1971 I was essentially the same weight I am now with a BMI in the normal range. (Was that before BMI?) I knew I had a problem with food because I spent so much time thinking about it: how to get it, how to prepare it, how always to have enough, and how to get rid of the debris related to my excessive eating of it. The rest of the time I spent thinking about how to starve myself, how to make the scale say something other than what it said, and how to find a way to eliminate those parts of me I disliked (hips, thighs, love handles, lap overs, and buttocks.)

Some of you may recognize the time of "Twiggy" when I had a "Jlo" body. A long time ago. I no longer have a body like that one. Oh, well.

In the years in between, I took a 100-pound bite. (What this means: I got angry with someone and broke my abstinent behavior by eating something not on my agreed upon plan of eating. Then I proceeded to EAT. I gained a pound or a pound and a half every month for eight years. Eventually, I had gone from 124 pounds to over 224 pounds. On my five feet 4 ½ inch body, that was excessive!) I struggled to reduce the poundage which damaged metatarsals in my feet. I experienced mental, emotional, spiritual, and physical distress; however, today I do have a body I love to live in. My brain no longer attacks me (well, not often.) I have clarity of mind. I have relationships I cherish. I have a life way beyond my wildest dreams.

So, how do you get from suffering from X (fill in the blank) to freedom? Turn it all upside down? Intrigued? This book is for you.

I will share with you examples of what is now called by a variety of names: food addiction, food dependency, food allergies, disordered eating, anorexia, bulimia, binge eating disorder, compulsive eating, food as a substance use disorder, and eating addiction. There are other names. Some of the writers included will call their relationship with substance X by a different name than the one you might use; however, please read and consider.

Do you have the problems they had?

Do you want a solution? Might their solutions work for you?

Would several aspects hooked together give you a solution to your issues?

I'm sharing this book and the information in it with you. In the table of contents, you'll find a variety of resources. Some may choose to read from beginning to end. Others may dip into various chapters that seem most important. Come back to read those that you missed initially if the ones you do read seem helpful to you.

If you are a professional, the materials may be helpful for you and your clients or patients. You might read the material as though for yourself first and then for your clients or your patients first and then for yourself. Please consider this information from a personal view as well as a professional view. A Wise One once said, "We teach best that which we most need to learn."

Before we continue, let us consider one question more: is there any food that I have difficulty controlling? *Yes, carbs*

That simple question added to health practitioners' repertoires regarding smoking, alcohol consumption, etc. might serve as the beginning of the revolution in healthcare. If each of us sees a difficulty controlling a specific food or category of foods or several foods or beverages, the next question is what can I do about it? And the answer often is "I've tried everything."

The "Everything I've tried," might not have included abstinence from grain, sugar, and alcohol or other specifics in your case. In the Alcoholics Anonymous Big Book, Dr. Silkworth in the Doctor's Opinion states, "This phenomenon {of craving}... may be the manifestation of an allergy which differentiates these people, and sets them apart as a distinct entity. It has never been, by any treatment with which we are familiar permanently eradicated. The only relief we have to suggest is entire abstinence." (pg. xxvi, 2001) He spoke of alcohol. Today, I might offer you the opportunity to see MRIs that suggest that sugar consumption (and its close cousin grain) may, in fact, have the same brain chemistry effects as alcohol and cocaine.

Thus, the solution I suggest is entire abstinence from grain, sugar, and alcohol. Those who have repeatedly tried anything less have failed as often as they tried, as did I. The reason for this is fear; a re-creation of fears of the past, sometimes long past, sometimes historically or genetically past, but nevertheless in our own personal experience. I will not starve. I will not be hungry. I will eat bountiful, abundant, spectacularly colorful diverse proteins, oils, fruits, and vegetables. I will eat without shame or guilt and without fear for the first time in life. Freedom is available here now.

The stories included are those of professionals in the field of food addiction and obesity as well as those of "ordinary" people in diverse parts of the world and in varied careers with different periods of struggle and abstinence.

If you identify similarities instead of differences, you may find our successes become more readily available to you. You may not need to repeat the same failures some of us report. You could save yourself years of exploration attempting to identify abstinence of varied kinds to give you the freedom you desire.

This book is a beginning. The purpose is to share the stories of those who have already identified themselves as having one of the labels listed above and to invite others to share their stories and their solutions. (That is an invitation to you.)

This book will offer you questions to aid you in assessing where you are at the beginning and later in different stages of your process. If you are willing to share your answers and changes with the authors, please do so.

If you are willing to share your struggles and successes with other readers, another book will make that possible. Please consider participating and either copy the pages of questions and your answers and then email them to us or go to our online site to share the answers, if you wish. Please choose and use a distinctive identifier to capture and connect the different parts of your process and success. Keep the distinctive identifier in case you want to add to your story of recovery.

There is a solution for you.

The only **challenges** are *identifying the solutions* which work for you and then *staying with the solutions* long enough to register the freedoms which exist while *continuing* to apply *consistently* the solutions you identify and new ones you may need.

Maymie Porter, an educator I never knew, is reputed to have asked three questions:

1. What did you like about what you did?
2. What would you change if you were to do it again?
3. What resources do you need?

I suggest you consider these questions as you proceed.

Credentials: first what I am not: I am not a licensed nutritionist or a dietitian. I am not an MD. I am not your therapist. I am not a person who has all the answers.

What I am is a person who has some answers (which work for me.) I have a doctorate in education and decades of experience teaching kindergarteners through adults. I have other licensing and degrees not all of which are pertinent here.

I have studied with the Institute of Integrative Nutrition, IIN; ACORN, ACORN Food Dependency Recovery Services; the Florida School of Addiction Studies; INFACT, the International School for Food Addiction, Counseling, and Treatment; and SUGAR, Sugar Use General Assessment Recording (a structured evaluation instrument built on ICD-10/International Classification of Diseases and Related Health Problems from WHO) criteria for alcohol and drug addiction and is adapted for pathological use of sugar/flour/food.

Most importantly, I have personal experience attempting, struggling, and succeeding in the last 48 years dealing with each of the X factors listed above. I have successes to share. Some of these are my own; others are those of friends and colleagues who are willing to share with you.

What will you find in this book?

1. References to definitions others have offered.
2. A questionnaire for each reader to consider his or her own awareness and potentially to share with the authors for future collaborative resources for even greater numbers of travelers on the path of blissful, contented and purposeful lives.
3. Individual stories of experiences with food allergies and addictions.

4. A list of potential resources to explore.
5. The eating plans which may remove the more common allergies and addictions.
6. An invitation to give feedback on the eating plan you choose.
7. An invitation to share your examples of food allergies and addictions which might assist others, their doctors, their nutritionists and dietitians, and other health practitioners.
8. A new definition and methods to use to identify and choose what works for you.
9. Methods to maintain behaviors which support your well-being.

My colleague Dave Avram Wolfe and I offer you a strategy to identify and address potential changes in two areas each week for the duration of the time it takes to read all of the material in the book and to make the changes you want to make in your own life while assisting others possibly to do the same in their lives.

Tuesday 10:00 a.m.

HOW TO USE RESOURCES IN THIS BOOK

We invite you to consider creating a mini social support group: this could be you and another friend who then each invite another one or two to share in a session two personal goals weekly. Please obtain a notebook in which to keep your answers to questions asked. Each of the group members makes a commitment to the group to participate actively in change efforts and to support the others in their attempts. Reporting the outcomes of the previous week while making two new commitments for the coming week will take most of the time for each session while continuing to read from the text and to share on individual's identification with the reading.

A-Team. Abstinence

You can be a part of the ABSTINENCE-Team or A-Team. Abstinence usually requires extraordinary support. Weekly, we will be using A's to create an optimal environment for abstinence. Alpha, Aim, Awareness, Abstinence, Actions, Accountability, Acceptance, Appreciation, Assessment and "A Gain" will focus the group's sharing and work as we move through the process of obtaining and maintaining abstinence from foods and/or behaviors.

If you always wanted to achieve A's in school, now is the time to do it. Dedicate your time and energy to outstanding success on the goals of each week, the ones you have chosen for yourself. One circuit speaker in a 12-step program often stressed using the steps as though your life depends on them, for it does. In this program, you might identify your goals as ones your heart desires. To achieve the goals weekly may determine the rest of your life.

Give your best effort and achieve those As you always wanted and deserved. You can then model for those you love the Abstinence-Team/ A-Team spirit and accomplishments you have personally achieved. Then you will not be saying, "Do this because I said so." Instead, you will calmly and directly acknowledge, "If I can do this, you can too, if you are willing to attempt joining the A-team to gain the support you need to succeed. You can do this."

Week One: Alpha

AGENDA for the FIRST MEETING

The following might be an agenda for the **first meeting**:

- Introduction of who I am and why I chose to participate in this session.
- What is it I hope to achieve during the weeks of the reading and commitment sharing in this process?
- What specific goals am I considering related to food consumption, weight, health, and well-being?
- What additional areas of change might serve me well?

Each group member might take 10 minutes to complete an introduction. A review of the process for creation of SMARTEST GOALS.

Using THE SMARTEST GOALS model, **each group member creates two goals for the week to come. One of the goals will perhaps include reading and considering the eating plan offered by Dave Avram Wolfe.** What changes will be necessary to try out the food plan for this week and the remaining weeks of reading the stories?

Another goal might include any other behavior **not** food related.

Often in the first week, cleaning out the cupboards and refrigerator comprise an example of this goal.

Noticing what one eats and writing down every bite with the time of eating and then the results (hunger, cravings, gas, bloating, fear, hives, rosacea, obsessive thoughts, lust, relaxation, pleasure,) and the time those experiences occurred might be an additional first week goal.

Some areas others have chosen for *a goal unrelated to food* might include having more fun or clearing away one area of clutter daily.

Noting the time spent practicing meditation with or without an app might be another goal area.

Another example might be creating a baseline for any change of behavior in a positive direction (increased minutes on a treadmill or number of steps on an app for increasing steps or increasing or decreasing numbers of hours of sleep to attain 7-9 hours per night in a consistent waking and sleeping pattern.)

No matter whether the specific goal is related to food or to another area of endeavor, the goals are constructed as SMARTEST GOALS. Please read the instructions during the first session and practice with the aid of your co-collaborators to create workable goals for yourselves. The clearer and more precise your goals are, the more likely each is to be accomplished.

Success brings success. Those unable to succeed at their goals for the week may need more specificity in goal setting. Sometimes, making smaller goals to create Swiss cheese holes in the larger goal serves. Sometimes, extraordinary support may be needed to complete the goals for subsequent weeks. More about that later.

Smart goals are available on the Internet with numerous explanations.
Smarter goals, likewise. Smartest goals:

S - Specific:

Who?
What?
When?
Where?
And why?
These questions if answered will provide the best goals

M - Measurable:

How will you be able to know if you have succeeded or not?
How many times?
How much?
How many?
Be specific.

A - Agreed:

With whom do you need agreements?
Family?
Close friends?
A support group or groups?
Oneself?
A spiritual commitment or covenant?

R - Realistic:

Achievable and demanding but not impossible within the time frame (next step.)

T - Time Defined:

You commit to complete this goal by when?
Be specific as this confines the unending possibilities!
Different goals may have different time frames allowed for completion. Making "Swiss Cheese commitments" (i.e., smaller holes in a larger goal) make accomplishments more accessible.

E - Ethical:

Living with your highest ethical standards supports success. This is quite individual; however, your collaborative intention to support your of their goal.

S - Succinctly Recorded:

The goal written down in brief sentences makes it available for review, evaluation, and celebration when completed.

T - Thought Out Carefully:

We often achieve our goals and then find there were missing pieces. Be attentive to what you seek for you may be successful! (At one time my husband and I were seeking homeownership near the Pacific or the Atlantic Oceans; however, we frequently talked about it as living near "water." When we found our new condo, it was overlooking Lake Michigan, which is water and appears to be an ocean! Were we successful?)

So, practice making your SMARTEST GOALS: one for food for this week and one which is directed at some other area of your life.

Goals often start with letting go of that which is excess or is not needed, like the quote describing chipping away all that was not needed. The quote is attributed to Michelangelo.[1] I heard the story from Smokey Newton, a Sunset Boulevard sculptor and jeweler who saw in a log beside his driveway "Big Girl," and then he chipped away everything that was not Big Girl.

Other goals require the acquisition of habits and behaviors which will "push out" the negatives with new positives. We have resources: "time, talent and treasure."[2] How might I best use these precious resources? (For just a moment, think back 5 years or 10 years or 20 years. That quickly, the past has become where and who and what we are now. Ask yourself the following questions: "How quickly will the next 5 or 10 or 20 years pass? Where do I want to be? How might I get there? Is today the day to begin letting go of the unnecessary and acquiring the skill sets to achieve my SMARTEST GOALS?"

Hoping your answer to the last question is a loud affirmative!

Today is the day, the only day we have. As you probably have heard, it is "the present." Let each of us enjoy the gift. Tomorrow will be a new present. We do not ever know how many days we will have. Enjoy this one. Use your creativity to make the goals to succeed in enjoying new and precious days one day at a time.

Week Two: Aim

INTRODUCTION of an EATING PLAN

Food: what is food and what does it mean for us individually and collectively as a society or culture?

Food for thought: what does this phrase mean and how can I use it as I progress through this book?

---

[1]   https://quoteinvestigator.com/2014/06/22/chip-away/

[2]   http://www.stfranciswichita.com/index.php/stewardship/time-talent-treasure

Eating: what is eating and when something is eating me how does that change my eating?

Choosing an eating plan: from all the myriad eating plans available: what one is right for me? What ones have I already tried? Which ones worked and for how long? What aspects seem to have worked the best? Might I take these into consideration as I make commitments to change my eating and other behaviors and thinking now?

Underpinnings for food changes include an eating plan that works to remove toxins from the brain and body. For many this is a step-by-step process. For those suffering from the phenomenon of craving, the most common trigger to remove is sugar. The next most common and usually the one least recognized is grain. For some who have Caribbean heritage, fat might be included here. Fortunately for most of us, the exclusion of oil is not warranted but instead oil is a desirable substance in measured quantities.

Alcohol, generally made from grain and high sugar elements and then fermented, may be easy for some to forgo. For others, this may be a challenge. If it seems impossible or unnecessary to forgo imbibing, an additional step may be necessary. Alcohol is a trigger for many who have food allergies or respond emotionally to food. If one cannot stop imbibing, attendance at six open to the public Alcoholics Anonymous meetings may be useful.

For many who were involved with alcohol earlier in their lives, the absence of alcohol usually requires continuous support to maintain abstinence, especially when releasing sugar (etc.), the primary or first addiction for many.

For those who are grain and sugar addicted, additional continuous support to maintain abstinence may be needed as well.

Ask for what you need from group members, family, friends, and any other support groups you care to explore. 12 Step Programs are resources; however, numerous support groups exist. You may want to check out several.

A note on withdrawal symptoms

When one has experienced repeated contact with substances to which one responds negatively or one may believe positively, if that substance is removed, the body experiences withdrawal symptoms. These may include physical pain, nausea, anxiety, sleeplessness, and cravings. Some may have experienced these with the absence of caffeine or diet soda. It seems that the only solution is more caffeine and more diet soda. If attempts at moderation have failed, the solution is abstinence.

On a recent plane trip, I sat next to a medical doctor. As I often do, I shared the methods I have used to be free from substances and behaviors that plagued me. That doctor's request was for me to find something to address harm reduction rather than abstinence. I had experienced a similar conversation with another doctor earlier in my life. Harm reduction does help. For a time. For some people. If it works for you, do it. Harm reduction is not a solution for cravings. The only solution to cravings is abstinence from the substance craved.

I know it makes no sense. It makes no sense to the addicted brain. The addicted brain has been hijacked by the substances or behaviors creating the cravings. (The experience for 85 years of another abstaining society: AA shows abstinence from a substance works.)

A therapist suggested his clients make three lists:

1. 10 foods I love (prioritized from most loved = #1 to least loved #10)
2. 10 foods I can take or leave.
3. 10 foods I dislike.

The suggestion then was to stop eating the foods on list three; eat the foods as desired on list two; and begin by stopping eating the first item on the first list and working down from there. For most people that is an accurate solution. Try it.

(If you get cravings or withdrawal symptoms, you are on the right track. Continue. Drink plenty of water. Work up a sweat each day.

Avoid breaks or vacations from abstinence as those deplete stamina and initiate the return of cravings. Consistency one day at the time supports abstinence "muscle" building.

You too can gain success. The Twelve Steps program surrender and invite surrender to a Power Greater than Oneself. Usually the belief includes surrender to a Power which wants you free from addictive substances and behaviors. (That is a Higher Power or H.P. for many).

Consistency in maintaining "no matter what happens" attitude toward abstinence is a requisite to continuous abstinence. If you have had less than two years of abstinence previously, some would say you had not relapsed because you had not yet achieved abstinence of two years free from the substance or behavior. Some may choose "One Day At A Time: No Matter What" as a mantra to deal with continuity. This was and still is my personal practice while adding the H.P. most of the days.

A list of potential resources to explore:

Eating Plans in Public Media

Eating Plans from a Nutritionist

Eating Plans from a Dietitian

Eating Plans from a Doctor

Eating Plans from a Diet Company

Eating Plans from a Friend

Eating Plans from a Parent

Exercising More

12 Step Program

a.   Overeaters Anonymous
b.   OA- HOW (Honesty Openness and Willingness*)
c.   CEA HOW Compulsive Overeaters Anonymous-HOW*
d.   Food Addicts in Recovery
e.   Food Addicts Anonymous
f.   GreySheeters Anonymous
g.   Other (specify please)
h.   Other (specify please)

Online resources including Food Addiction Institute (foodaddictioninstitute. org; twitter, facebook, instagram) and You Tube resources there

An eating plan may serve to remove some of the more common allergies and addictions:

Eating Less of sugar and grain (least likely success for addicts)

Eating More and excluding White Sugar and White Flour

Eating More and excluding Sugar

Eating More and excluding Grain

Eating More and excluding all Grains and Sugars

Eating More and excluding all your individual trigger foods

If you are working by yourself through this book, share your goals with a friend or partner. If you choose to form a group, you and a friend might each invite one or two others to join you in committing to read and use this resource together. Make your determination now and decide by what date and time you will meet on the phone, on zoom or skype, or in person in a quiet place.

As a group, identify your goals by using the process above. Together, please do this for the group and then each participant may continue the process one by one to have specific personal

goals. As group goals are formulated, some groups include parameters for respectful treatment of an individual's personal goals. We not only agree to the goals set by the individual, but we also assume an attitude of acceptance and support for change which may be most helpful.

One suggestion is to have each group member share two goals weekly: one which has to do with food and food consumption and a second goal with a different behavior, unrelated to food. These might include changes (increases and decreases) in behaviors re spending, working, playing, decluttering, smoking, use and behaviors including gambling, spending, MORE or creativity, play, and mindfulness.

In addition to reading sections of the book and discussing them, you might include what resonates with each participant, reporting on specific goals from the last week and committing to specific goals for the future week. These will usually complete the time allowed for the group. Depending upon the size of the group this may be a committed hour or hour and a half weekly until the modules and the book headings are completed. Plus, one additional meeting for closure or new commitments.

Definitions others have put forward:

If you are interested in the defintion the DSM and ICD are the official definitions by the medical community in the US and the World Health Organisation (WHO).

https://www.psychiatry.org/psychiatrists/practice/dsm
https://www.who.int/classifications/icd/en/

Dr. Vera Tarman is a medical practitioner with a specialty in addiction medicine. The following sections are adapted from *Food Junkies: The Truth About Food Addiction*. Published by Dundurn Press, Nov 2014 and are used with her permission.

Dr Vera Tarman has been working in the field of addiction medicine since 1994. She became accredited with the Board of Addiction Medicine (ABAM) in 2004. She has been the medical director of Renascent since 2006. She is a regular contributor to the call-in TV show *Living Clean, Living Well* and was cohost on *Addictions Unplugged*, a community call-in show about addictions.

Although she has spoken on various issues in addiction, her special interest is the area of food addiction. She is the author of *Food Junkies: The Truth about Food Addiction*. Dr Tarman has found working at Renascent extremely rewarding, mainly because of its support of an abstinence model of care and its acceptance that the spiritual as well as medical and psychological dimensions are important for recovery. Dr Tarman and Renascent believe that good care involves treating addiction *and* fostering a lifelong recovery life plan based on community and peer support. The power is ours!

(Bio taken from Addictions Unplugged)

ARE YOU A FOOD ADDICT? A CHECKLIST

Dr. Vera Tarman, MD, M.Sc., FCFP, CASAM, ABAM Diplomate

- Have you ever wanted to stop eating and found you just couldn't?
- Do you think about food or your weight constantly?
- Do you find yourself attempting one diet or food plan after another with no lasting success?
- Do you binge and then "get rid of the binge" through vomiting, exercise, laxatives or another form of purging?
- Do you eat differently in private than you do in front of people?
- Do you eat to escape your feelings?
- Do you eat when you're not hungry?
- Have you ever discarded food, only to retrieve and eat it later?
- Do you fast or severely restrict your food intake?
- Have you ever stolen other people's food?
- Have you ever hidden food to make sure you have "enough?"
- Do you obsessively calculate the calories you've burned against the calories you've eaten?
- Do you frequently feel guilty or ashamed about what you've eaten?
- Do you feel hopeless about your relationship with food?

If you have answered yes to more than three of these questions, you could be a food addict. And if you can relate to the following conversation, typical of ones I have often with my patients, it may provide further proof:

Client: "Yesterday I ate all day long. I started with breakfast—a big three-cheese omelet, home fries, six pieces of toast. Then I had two raisin bagels with cream cheese, six chocolate-glazed doughnuts with a pint of milk and something else, I can't even remember what. For lunch I wanted to eat something 'normal,' so I went to a buffet and ate a salad loaded with cheese and cold cuts and tons of blue-cheese dressing with bacon bits. In the afternoon I had five or six candy bars, a bag of corn chips and a couple of granola bars. I went home and passed out but later went out for pizza.

Counselor: "When do you think you lost control?

Client: "The minute I got out of bed. I told myself I wasn't going to eat sugar, because sugar really sets me off, but it was like I was two people in one body. No matter what I said to myself, I picked up the food. I had one voice telling me to go ahead and one voice telling me not to."

AM I REALLY A FOOD ADDICT?
HOW CAN I TELL?

People claim to be addicted to everything from romance novels to cars. Office workers of normal weight sheepishly say they are addicted to cookies if they take the last Oreo from the break room. Women who enjoy the occasional plate of pasta turn to their partners and say, "I wish I wasn't so addicted to spaghetti." But are they clinically addicted?

Although abnormal eating behaviors have been identified throughout history, until recently scientists and clinicians alike have been reluctant to acknowledge that food addiction exists. Some outright deny it. My colleague and collaborator, Phillip Werdell, a soft-spoken 70-year-old, is part of a group of professionals dedicated to improving our understanding of food as an addictive substance. His views on the subject are militant.

"The position that there is no scientific evidence supporting food addiction flies in the face of research gathered over the past 15 years," he says. "There are well-designed animal experiments, detailed brain imaging studies and more than 3,000 peer-reviewed papers[3]. Unsupported criticism is just plain anti-science and anti-intellectual, much like the debunking of global warming. If it looks like an addiction and responds to treatment like an addiction, then why not call it an addiction?"

A rise in overeating over the past 30 years corresponds to the supersizing trend in restaurant meals and fast food containers as well as the

---

[3] www.foodaddictioninstitute.org/FAI-DOCS/Full-bibliography.pdf

processed-food industry's research that has helped it to exponentially increase the reward potency of foods. Gradually the public is coming to accept food addiction as a disorder but we clinicians working in this field are impatient with the pace of change. Until the medical community acknowledges this diagnosis, the identification and treatment of food addiction remains hampered.

HOW DO WE DIAGNOSE FOOD ADDICTION?

As food addiction becomes accepted as a medical condition, it is necessary to develop a method of diagnosing it. So far, there is no lab test to determine if a person has any addiction, let alone a complex one like food addiction. Over the past five years alone, innovations in neurological radiology, like functional MRIs and SPECT scans, have allowed scientists to strongly suggest a link between our brain's propensity for addiction and food. Within the next decade, we can expect physicians to find external markers to determine addiction in the same way we expect to diagnose clinical depression or ADHD.

Today, however, we base our diagnosis of addiction mainly on questions and observations. The questionnaire I presented at the beginning of this article is part of the toolkit used by several 12-step food addiction programs[4]. If you answered yes to just a few of the questions, you may be a food addict. But until there is an official diagnosis, clinicians usually apply to food the American Psychiatric Association's *Diagnostic and Statistical Manual of Mental Disorders (DSM-V)* criteria for general addiction (under the category "substance abuse disorder").

The DSM-V provides guidelines for clinicians to follow when making a psychiatric diagnosis. A patient has a substance abuse dependency if he or she has developed distress associated with three or more of the following seven markers within a 12-month period:

- Patient has developed a tolerance or withdrawal symptoms
- Patient has developed persistent cravings for the substance
- Patient has frequently taken more of the substance than planned

---

[4] https://foodaddictioninstitute.org/

- Patient has taken excessive time acquiring, using or recovering from the effects of the substance
- Patient continues to use the substance despite difficulties
- Patient has given up work, social or family activities if they interfere with using the substance
- Patient has made multiple attempts to cut down on use of the substance

The single most important feature leading physicians to suspect addiction is that patients experience cravings and obsessions surrounding their drug of choice. For food addicts, cravings are typically focused on foods that are high in sugar and fat: the muffin for breakfast, the latte loaded with sugar and cream at lunch, the apple cruller on the way home from work. Anyone can look forward to a snack but food addicts think about their favourite foods all day. They sometimes begin thinking about their next snack before they've finished the one they're eating. Large amounts of even the healthiest of food can overwhelm the body's hormonal regulation and satiation signals. One client of mine would munch through three large bags of carrots a day, eating so many that her skin turned an orange hue.

Withdrawal symptoms are another key sign of addiction. Recovering from a food "hangover" can last for days. Critics often use this criterion as their proof that food addiction doesn't exist; they insist that there is no measurable physical withdrawal from a food binge equivalent to the DTs, seizures, goose bumps and diarrhea associated with alcohol or drugs. I have to wonder if these critics have ever asked a person who has just binged on 5,000 calories of sugar and fat how they feel the next morning? I've witnessed withdrawal symptoms—not seizures, true, but snappy moods, insomnia, tremors, nausea, aching muscles and a mental fog that can be as dramatic as any alcohol hangover....

Just as alcoholics waste inordinate time hiding bottles and planning opportunities for swigs, food addicts can spend hours plotting their days around meals and snack times. (More time may be wasted counting calories and excessively exercising.) They may get through the morning by promising themselves a pizza at lunchtime and get through the afternoon thinking about a tub of caramel ice cream they'll have at night. Some food addicts are "grazers," constantly eating handfuls of peanuts, a bag of jelly beans, a buttered bagel, a banana...; others are "binge eaters," consuming large quantities of food in one sitting. Either way, food helps quell distressing feelings, soothe anxieties, numb emotional pain. The depression and shame can take days to dissipate, and any of these feelings are a red flag indicating addiction.

Make no mistake, like any addict [sic] food addicts intuitively know they're engaging in self-destructive behaviour. They know friends and family members are concerned, and their physicians have counseled them to lose weight. How can they live with this ongoing anguish? The food addict's system of denial becomes ever more complex and defensive as the addiction progresses and they reach for even more bizarre rationalizations: *The diabetes isn't that bad yet. I can get away with binging one last time. I may as well go all out since I blew it today anyway.* These are typical examples of what's known as "stinking thinking."

The mainstay of addiction is an inability to stop, despite repeated efforts. How many dieters do you know who have attempted to stop or cut back and been successful over the long term? They start off with the best intentions to cut back on portions of bread and pasta, but eventually return to eating these foods, sometimes in greater quantities; they try to have just one cookie but eat the whole bag. The true food addict simply can't stop, not for long. Willpower is no match for the overwhelming obsessive desire to eat.

To access 3,000 peer-reviewed writings, see https://www.foodaddictioninstitute.org

For more recent research: https://foodaddictioninstitute.org/resources/books-and-publications/research/

Take a Quiz to determine if someone is a food addict: https://foodaddictioninstitute.org/quiz/

SIDEBAR: A brief history of food addiction

- In 1960, an overweight woman named Rozanne S. founded the 12-step fellowship, Overeaters Anonymous, after recognizing that her overeating was similar to a friend's uncontrollable gambling addiction. After attending a Gamblers Anonymous meeting, she wrote in her memoir, *Beyond Our Wildest Dreams: A History of Overeaters Anonymous as Seen by a Cofounder*, "Our compulsions were not the same. They were obsessed with gambling and money and I thought of nothing but overeating and food. Still, inside we were the same."

- William Dufty's 1975 bestseller, *Sugar Blues*, made the case that sugar is an addictive substance that can be compared to drugs such as opium, morphine and heroin. He had no peer-reviewed literature, no double-blind studies, no MRIs or PET scans to back up his claims, only his own history and that of other believers who felt unhealthy and out-of-control when they ate sugar.

- In 1981, a 29-year-old woman unable to stop binging on food approached a respected alcohol rehabilitation facility for help. After describing her behaviour to the intake team the surprised head of the facility remarked, "That sure sounds like alcoholic behaviour to me." She was admitted on an experimental basis, since the team had never treated anyone addicted to food. Her counsellor advised that whenever she heard the word "alcohol" to replace it in her mind with "food."

- In 1985, Judi Hollis' *Fat is a Family Affair: How Food Obsessions Affect Relationships* was published. Originally Hollis' Ph.D. dissertation, it included for the first time legitimate academic research about food addiction.

• A year later, a Florida-based psychiatric hospital called Glenbeigh opened a companion unit to its drug and alcohol rehab centre devoted to treating food addiction and eating disorders. (It quickly earned a reputation as the best residential facility in the world.) In heartbreaking detail, patients described stealing food, taking it from the trash, getting stopped by police while driving and eating, blacking out after overeating and eating beyond the pain of a distended stomach only to resume binging after the pain subsided. Collectively, patients had gained and lost hundreds of thousands of pounds and spent untold sums of money on food, diet drugs and weight loss schemes. Many had thought about, or attempted, suicide.

• In 1993, mental health counselor Kay Sheppard published a revised version of her signature work, *Food Addiction: The Body Knows*. Drawing from her experience working with food addicts, she didn't mince words: "Food addiction is a chronic, progressive and ultimately fatal disease. It is chronic because the condition never goes away, progressive because the symptoms get worse over time and fatal because those who persist in the disease will die an early death due to its complications."

• Nora D. Volkow, director of the Maryland-based National Institute on Drug Abuse (NIDA), was among the first to begin connecting the dots between food abuse and other addictions. She was instrumental in having food classified with the plethora of other addictions that American physicians were responsible for treating. Writing in the scientific journal *Nature Neuroscience* in 1995, Volkow highlighted studies linking dopamine levels in compulsive overeaters and cocaine addicts. Among other findings, she cited brain studies that recorded dopamine increases in humans who simply *looked at* images of food. Volkow wrote: "In some obese individuals, the loss of control and compulsive food taking behavior share characteristics with the compulsive drug intake observed in drug-addicted subjects."

- In 2009, Dr. Dave A. Kessler, former commissioner of the U.S. Food and Drug Administration, published *The End of Overeating: Taking Control of the Insatiable American Appetite.* Echoing Volkow, Kessler shared his experiential evidence on the addictive nature of food as well as scientific studies explaining the brain chemistry behind food cravings and compulsive eating. Kessler stopped short of calling the phenomenon an addiction, opting instead for the term "conditional hypereating."

- Finally, in 2011, the American Society of Addiction Medicine (ASAM) redefined the nature of addiction itself. No longer a matter of poor choice or weak emotional control, the ASAM officially defined food addiction as a brain disorder. Its conclusion: While willpower plays a role in curbing the behaviours endemic to addiction, it is the smallest factor. "At its core, addiction isn't just a social problem or a moral problem or a criminal problem," says Dr. Michael Miller, past-president of ASAM who oversaw the new definition. The disease "is about brains, not drugs. It's about underlying neurology."

Thank you to Dr. Vera Tarman for these insights.

INTRODUCTION TO A METHOD
FOR SHARING YOUR STORY

An invitation to give feedback on the eating plans: If you choose to try one of the following eating plan, what observations have you? Please share what works and what does not work for you.

An invitation to share your examples of food allergies and addictions which might assist others, their doctors, and their dietitians, nutritionists, and other health practitioners. What is your story? We want to share recovery stories. Are you willing to share yours?

A new definition and methods to use to choose what works for you.

1. Am I hungry two hours after I eat X?

2. Do I experience withdrawal symptoms after X?

   a. Hunger
   b. Inflammation
   c. Aching joints
   d. Brain Fog
   e. Headaches
   f. Sinus congestion
   g. Itching
   h. Skin rashes
   i. Other (please identify)

3. Do I try to delay eating until later?

4. Do I graze (eat throughout waking hours)?

5. Do I sleep 8 hours most nights?

6. Do I drink 8 glasses of water most days?

7. Do I eat at least 3-4 hours before I sleep?

8. Do I take a daily multivitamin?

9. Do I take supplements?

10. If so, what?

11. Do I exercise most days? If so what? How many steps? How long?

12. Do I engage in some spiritual or mindfulness practices most days?

13. What else do I need to be free of my addictions?

14. What kind of support has helped me in the past?

15. How much support do I need?

16. How much support and what kinds of support am I willing to accept?

    Phone, Face to Face, Commitments (of what and how often), Retreats, Service, Helping Others, Journaling, Writing Inventories, Writing MY Story, Sharing Descriptions of Success and Incidents in which I was less successful, Slips, Avalanches, Hopes, Dreams, Bookending, Therapy, In House Treatment, Outpatient Treatment, One at a Time Releases of Addictions, Full Out Across the Board Putting Down All Addictions at the Same Time (or something in between)?

17. What foods do I know cause me challenges?

18. In what categories are these foods: Proteins, Carbohydrates, Fats, Sugars, Grains, Salt, Spices?

19. What Flavors are challenges: Sweet, Umami (Savory), Sour, Bitter, Salty

20. What Textures are Challenges? Soft, Mushy, Crunchy, Gooey, Chewy, Crispy

21. Do I have a list of 100 things to do instead of picking up food? (Do I use the list?)

22. Do I have recipes that are quick and easy to use?

23. Do I wait at least 4 hours between meals?

24. Do I brush my teeth after each meal?

25. Do I have abstinent labeled frozen portions in the freezer ready to take with me when I am in a hurry?

26. Do I plan my meals and my sleeping hours first and <u>then</u> the rest of my day?

27. Do I weigh out my food to determine what I am eating actually?

28. Do I have a device to keep track of important aspects of my daily health plan? (food choices, sleep, steps, water, etc.)

29. Do I snore loudly?

30. If I am not sleeping well have I talked with a doctor re a sleep study?

31. If I have hot flashes, have I contacted a hormone specialist for assessment for bioidentical hormones?

32. If I have cravings, have I begun to abstain from those foods <u>and</u> their cousins?

33. How many days does my detox take?

34. How long have I been dependent on these foods or behaviors?

35. What is my earliest memory of using these foods or behaviors?

36. What was the emotional milieu in which I engaged with these foods or behaviors?

37. Have friends, family, and medical practitioners suggested I eat specific foods more moderately?

38. What were the outcomes?

Please send your story for The Fix For Cravings to <u>TheFixforCravings@gmail.com</u> <u>LightOfCindy@wordpress.org</u> for blogs by Cynthia, <u>David@triggerfreenutrition.com</u> for blogs by Dave and <u>www.triggerfreenutrition.com</u>

GETTING FREE FROM TRIGGER FOODS

DAVE AVRAM WOLFE'S PERSPECTIVE

I have come into the field of food addiction quite honestly. I grew up with two food addicts in my immediate family and encountered many others in my extended family. As a child I remember my grandfather polishing off half a large pizza at the kitchen counter and then sitting down and asking my grandmother, "Charlotte, what is for supper?" This exposure, at such a young age, provides me with the insight and understanding to work with food addicts today.

I have found that most clinicians know very little about food addiction and about the treatment of substance addiction in general. In the Western medical community, the concept of being addicted to certain foods/eating is considered quite preposterous and ridiculous.

As a Registered Dietitian (RD) and Food Addiction Counselor (FAC), I have found a couple of ways to deal with this. My first approach is to talk about food addiction as if there is absolutely no doubt that it is a disease which impacts many lives. When I first started my work in weight management, I made it my mission to simply use food addiction related terminology in my notes as well as when raising concerns to the physicians with whom I work. Within six months I began seeing the following comments in their notes and emails: "Client instructed to talk to Dave about food addiction." or "Food addiction may be present." Even on a small scale, I consider this a major victory. My second approach is to not waste time trying to persuade non-believers. It is too exhausting. This fatigue prevents me from supporting those I could otherwise help. Instead, I focus my time and energy on the clinicians open to the idea or those *willing* to be open to the idea of food addiction.

I use the word "insidious," defined as "proceeding in a gradual subtle way, but with harmful effects", to describe the type of disease food addicts are battling. The food addict believes, "This time it will be different, and this time I will stop after one serving." However, time and time again he discovers this is impossible, and the harmful effects of the use and abuse of the substance continue to get worse, never better. This ist just like alcoholism or any other substance or behavioral addiction.

In *Staying Sober A Guide to Relapse Prevention,* authors Gorski and Miller state, "Addiction is a condition in which a person develops bio-psycho-social dependence on a mood-altering substance." I believe it is not only a *substance,* but it can also be a *behavior.* In the case of food addiction, the addictive *substance* is food or food like substances/ingredients and the physical motion of eating is the addictive *behavior.* The food addicted person uses food to relieve their pain and emotional suffering. Having eaten, the addict seeks more food to relieve the pain caused by his actions. The continued use of food leads to continued use of food.

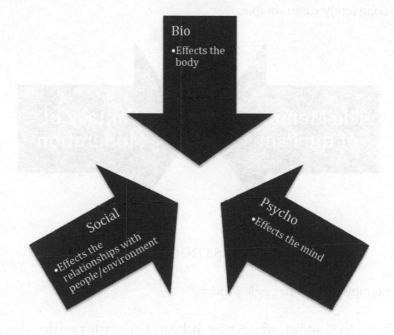

IMPLICATIONS OF ADDICTION

I believe we can better understand addictive behavior by viewing it through these two paradigms: **The Fantasy of Moderation vs. The Memory of the Pain**.

First, *The Fantasy of Moderation* encompasses the addict's inability to understand if the triggering substance is ingested, he will not be able to control the quantity of its intake. Second, it encompasses the addict's inability to avoid ingesting a triggering substance regardless of previous knowledge gained through his experiences. The first bite will lead to uncontrolled use. It is a ridiculous and unattainable goal for an addict to moderate intake, but the insidiousness of the disease provides the addict with the false hope of being able to do so.

On the other side we have *The Memory of the Pain*. This is a personal tool created by the addict who is in recovery. It is a memory based on healthy fear which is visceral to the individual. As my colleague says, "Stephen King Scary!" This memory helps the addict to stay on the path of recovery by reinforcing the reality that moderation is impossible and completely unattainable.

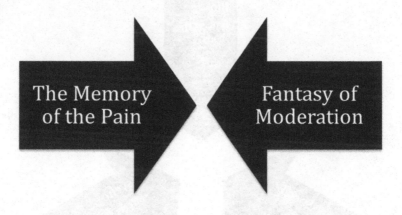

THE STRUGGLE

An example of this struggle follows:

Molly is a food addict, who is now diabetic. For nearly two decades, her doctor has been discussing her weight gain. She has been dieting for the past 25 years with no lasting effect on her weight, other than watching it slowly climb. Although the debilitating impact of the side effects of diabetes are looming in her future, already started on oral medications to help control her blood sugar, Molly continues to eat as before unable to change her diet. Even the idea of having to inject herself with insulin before bed and at meal times and the need to check her blood sugar five times per day have not kept her from eating and devouring her binge and trigger foods. Although these factors do scare Molly, they do not scare her **enough**. When Molly creates a vignette of her future health and the impact it will have on her husband and other family members, something begins to shift. What will happen when she is blind and in a wheelchair from years of poorly controlled blood sugar and terrible self-care? For Molly this creates a much stronger version of *The Memory of the Pain* because it involves **collateral damage**. It involves the people she loves, the people she cares for, and the people who will need to care for her. Now, *The Memory of the Pain* has become more visceral.

I encourage those I work with to find *The Memory of the Pain*, to continue to strengthen it and keep it sharp, and to carry it with them wherever they go. An example might be to keep an old cane in the trunk of your car to remember when you could not walk without it. However, if over time the power of this tool, the cane, becomes less strong and less visceral then you must strengthen your vignette. What if the cane becomes a wheelchair and you can't make it to your doctor's appointment alone? What if you require dressing changes on your legs and you can't bend over far enough to change them without assistance? What if you can no longer use the bathroom alone? These are just a few examples of strengthening *The Memory of the Pain* when *The Fantasy of Moderation* rears its ugly head. You now have the tools to slam the addiction back where it belongs—into the past!

Here are other examples of *The Memory of the Pain* I have heard from clients that may be helpful:

- Having to parent from the couch forever
- Needing to ask for the seat belt extender on an airplane
- Having to be airlifted off a cruise ship
- Not being able to leave the house or make it up or down the stairs

Most addicts, including food addicts, particularly those who are in early recovery or arc currently using or relapsing, experience shame or feelings of humiliation. The food addict uses binge foods and trigger foods in an attempt to remove these feelings. When they reoccur, the food addict ingests more of the same setting up a chronic cycle. Often in clinical practice, my clients will describe how some foods help them 'feel less sad,' while others 'take their pain away.' To help redirect their thinking, I often rephrase their statements. "What you are saying is that some foods are being used as antidepressants while other foods are being used as emotional or physical pain killers." This direct approach is often very helpful for individuals to realize how their *Fantasy of Moderation* is taking a very serious toll on their lives.

THE TRIGGER FREE FOOD TRIANGLE

This brings us to the next important concept and the cornerstone of my food addiction model: **The Trigger Free Food Triangle**. Using this tool will enable individuals to discover which foods are problematic. Over time we have come to the awareness that the foods which trigger us into excessive intake/restriction generally are involved with one, two or all three of the following concepts/emotions: *Debate*, *Guilt* **and/ or** *Romance*.

Debate: This is the element that takes place prior to the intake of a specific trigger food. It is the element that generally precedes guilt, but this is not always the case. I refer to debate as the grocery store dilemma. Typically, debate occurs long before we have the questionable food in our hands or even within sight. It is said, as human beings, we make over a thousand food decisions each day, and any one of these decisions could lead us back to debate. Let us look at the example of grocery shopping. Are you going to go straight to the vegetable section, or are you going to look at the bakery first? Is there anything on sale? What smells good? You turn, and you pass by the prepared foods, and you pass the chip aisle. What do you do? Do you dare enter the aisle? You know if you start to go down that aisle, you are going to have to deal with some serious will power. And you know will power hasn't worked for a very long time. You decide to enter the aisle, but you will only buy a baked chip product as an attempt at moderation. You head over to the baked chip section, but not fast enough to avoid daydreaming about what else you could be eating or bingeing on today. You find the baked chips and you notice there are many options. Some are more binge worthy to you than others. You end up settling for baked sour cream and onion chips, and you know they carry more calories than any other type of baked chip, but you reason it's okay because they are baked and that is the rule you set for yourself today. In your head, you did okay. You successfully did damage control, but this is only an attempt at moderating the amount of damage you will inflict on yourself during the upcoming pre-planned binge (romance, to come later.) This process could happen several times during your grocery store trip. Will I go down the cracker aisle, and if I do what will be the result? All these scenarios are very high in debate, and I argue that any food addicts have any level of debate over has absolutely no place in their food plan. In this context, debate could also be described as decisions leading them to future pain. The number one rule about debate is it will always precede the intake of a trigger food. That is not to say more debate will not take place during the intake of this food. Some examples might be, I will have one more handful of chips, or I will eat five chips every ten minutes, or maybe I will only eat one chip for each paragraph I read, or I will only dip every other chip in my onion dip. These are all attempts at fighting off the discomfort caused by debate. Seldom will they work. Debate is our futile attempt to play with our fantasy of moderation. There are two ways to remove oneself from debate. One is to avoid eating the foods which cause debate, and the other is to eat the foods and move into *Guilt.*

Guilt: The second corner of the *Trigger Free Food Triangle,* will take place during and/or after the intake of a trigger food. Thoughts occurring during the guilt phase often appear very similar to those during the debate phase. During a binge, one might alternate between debate and guilt. Guilt is often associated with shame and feelings of defeat: "Well, I opened the bag and I feel badly about that, so I might as well make the evidence disappear," or "I bought candy for the kids and I know it's not good for them so I might as well eat it," etc. It is not unusual for feelings of guilt to last a very long time into recovery. However, I believe a poster hanging in my office sums this up perfectly, "When you lose, don't lose the lesson." (Brown, 2012) Often these thoughts and occurrences of guilt and shame will strengthen our need for *Memory of the Pain* to better fight against our *Fantasy of Moderation.*

Romance: The third corner of the *Trigger Food Triangle* describes those foods which food addicts love, lust for, or have a secret romantic relationship with. The addict often plans out these foods in advance. They may be a specific holiday dish or a food addicts will go out of their way for. The addict may eat these foods in secret and/or destroy the evidence of their consumption. One example of this may be eating "take out" in the car blocks away from their residence, so the remains can be thrown away in a public trash can ensuring they won't be found out by their friends or family. Often romance is described as a secret lover or an abusive romantic partner. The French word *rendezvous* often paints the perfect picture as two star crossed lovers meet in secret to partake of each other's company. With one lover being the addict and the other lover being their food drug of choice. One of my clients described her relationship with ice cream as an almost sexual behavior, one which she does not enjoy but cannot refuse. "I always have at least two half-gallons of ice cream on hand. The first I will binge out of and the second I bury in the bottom of my chest freezer. After my binge, I will dig out the buried carton, and use it to replace the now almost empty container. Then, I will make sure to remove a scoop from the top, so it looks like that is all I ate. If I am too sick to eat it, I will put it into the sink and melt it with hot water, so there is very little evidence of my behavior. I will then purchase another one or two halfgallons of ice cream to place at the bottom of my freezer for my next binge. My husband has no idea I eat this way; I am ashamed! I know every time I eat ice cream, I spend more time burying and unburying my secret stash than I do eating it. I am almost to the point where I don't think moderation will ever work. I am abusing myself with ice cream."

I often use this analogy to help individuals differentiate among the corners of the *Trigger Free Food Triangle*: **Debate** *is playing with matches.* **Romance** *is seeing how close your fingers can get to the flames.* **Guilt** *is getting burned.*

By using the *Trigger Free Food Triangle*, it becomes much simpler to decipher the foods one must avoid completely. You will often find these foods contain many of the same ingredients and often are loaded with one or more (usually more) of the following: sugar, sweeteners (both natural or artificial), salt, wheat/flour, potato, corn, oils/fats and indecipherable ingredients. Everyone is different regarding sensitivities.

Some food addicts in long term recovery are able to eat whole grains, for instance, but are not able to eat items made with refined flours; others are not able to eat whole grain flours at all. Others avoid all grains but will eat sweet potatoes. Some will eat fruits at well, while others will eat only those fruits containing less sugar or have fruit only once per day. Other individuals only eat berries. I have found in my clinical experience that rather than playing this game it is much easier to remove potentially triggering foods, instead of attempting to discover the exact nature of our food triggers. Although it can be limiting, this avoids the arduous trial and error process. Why not go through withdrawal once, rather than alternately withdrawing and using while trying to figure out why your cravings are still present!

It took a family member nearly 15 years in food recovery to discover she was addicted to all forms of grain as well as sugar and flour. Since she discovered this 15 years ago, she has maintained her abstinence and weight loss one day at a time. The knowledge of and abstinence from her trigger foods have made all the difference.

CRACKING DENIAL

THE THOUGHT PROGRESSION TO ACCEPTANCE

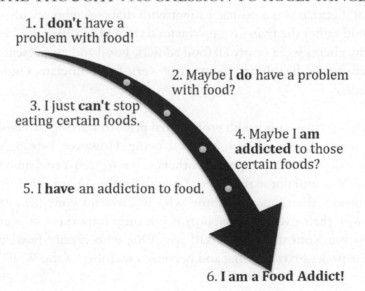

1. I **don't** have a problem with food!

2. Maybe I **do** have a problem with food?

3. I just **can't** stop eating certain foods.

4. Maybe I **am** addicted to those certain foods?

5. I **have** an addiction to food.

6. I am a **Food Addict!**

Paving The Road For Success

You will notice that *all* foods are to be weighed. There is no other accurate way to quantify food intake. Volume is simply inconsistent and inaccurate. One cup of green beans today may not weigh the same amount as one cup of green beans tomorrow. Depending on the cut or type, the volume may change. 8 oz. of green beans on a scale will always be 8 oz. of green beans on a scale. Period.

In my professional opinion, we need to take all the guesswork out of eating; we need black and white, crystal clear guidelines on how we are to eat as food addicts in long-term recovery. We must be able to tell when we are on and when we are off-plan. We must leave all our food decisions to the plan which will act as a road map and we must not waver from the plan. We have tried that thousands of times before and made little to no progress. Only in this way can we remove all the *debate, guilt, and romance* from our lives and leave our emotions for the people we interact with and not the foods we are addicted to.

Although I am a dietitian with extensive experience living with, and working with food addicts, I am not necessarily your dietitian. I remember when I worked in acute care, I would see hundreds of clients who were non-compliant diabetics. In fact, my very first patient as a student dietitian was a cardiac patient with diabetes who openly stated, "I would rather die than give up the foods that are killing me." I know now my clients were nearly all food addicts. Food addicts present a new problem to the healthcare system, one very few clinicians know how to handle.

Consulting with your health professional prior to starting this food plan is paramount for your health and well-being. However, I strongly urge you to also seek the support of others who are self-proclaimed food addicts. You will not make it very far without the support of your peers and without the support of those who understand your demons as if they were their own. Peer support is not only important; it is crucial. In isolation, your disease will kill you. One who cannot howl cannot find the pack...Start howling and become a member of the Wolfe Pack.

Before we dive headlong into the *Trigger Free Food Plans,* one more thing needs to be made perfectly clear. ***THIS IS NOT A DIET!*** Nor will it solve or cure food addiction without being paired with lifelong recovery and relapse prevention. ***THIS IS NOT A DETOX!*** This plan will **NOT** be slowly phasing back the foods it has removed from your life. That never has worked in the past with food addicts, and it certainly won't work now. If these foods were to be reintroduced, the cravings would return at once and in full force. Period. Then you will have to withdraw once more. Recovery from food addiction will become harder and harder as this cycle persists until death takes the addict or the addict finds long lasting recovery from this insidious, progressive, and deadly disease.

GETTING STARTED

Understanding The Basics Of The Trigger Free Food Plans

The logic that supports the framework of the *Trigger Free Low Carbohydrate Food Plan* and the *Trigger Free High Fat Low Carbohydrate Food Plan* is based on my understanding of nutritional science as well as my understanding of addiction. For the past five years I have worked as a registered dietitian, and more recently as a certified food addiction counselor treating food addicts in both private and medical sectors. As the new field of food addiction expands, so too will its options for treatments.

Before you blindly accept one of these plans as a lifelong journey of supporting your freedom from addiction to food, it is crucial to read, understand, and apply the following:

The *Trigger Free Food Plans* are based on **three** weighed and measured meals a day, breakfast lunch, and dinner. **Nothing is to be eaten between meals.** This allows for the stomach to digest and empty appropriately as well as to simplify and maintain food preparation. This may not be possible with a history of bariatric surgery. I encourage all food addicted bariatric surgery patients to work one on one with a trained food addiction clinician, such as myself, to create an individualized plan. This plan may include more than three meals.

The *Trigger Free Food Plans* are **sugar free**. Sugars are the simplest form of carbohydrates, which are known to be very addicting. If sugar is listed as one of the first four ingredients of a particular food item, it should not be eaten. It is particularly important to check the labels of salad dressings, marinades, sauces, and spice blends. **Note:** Sugar comes in many forms and has many names. (Appendix)

Sweeteners are not recommended. However, some food addicts have been unable to give up sugar without the use of sweeteners. Others, once their abstinence from sugar and grains was established, were then able to put them down. Consider the following analogy, as to why I strongly discourage their use. Dr. Nicole Avena, food addiction researcher in a webinar stated, "If sugar is Heroin, then sweeteners are Methadone." (Avena, 2017) If one examines the ingredients in sweeteners one will often find the first ingredient is either dextrose or maltose, which are both sugars. In my practice I have had food addicts with decades of abstinence from sugar and grains make the decision to give up artificial sweeteners. Many experienced excessive fatigue, headaches, irritability, and shakiness, which are all signs and symptoms of withdrawal. This leads me to believe that sweeteners are addictive and should be avoided. If they become problematic, they must be placed on your trigger list and be removed from your food plan.

The *Trigger Free Food Plans* are **grain free**. For these meal plans, grains will be defined as food products that can be refined or milled into starch or flour and/or foods that contain a high amount of carbohydrates (excluding fruit and specified beans). By this definition, the most common grains/starches include: wheat, rye, oats, barley, spelt, corn, potatoes, sweet potatoes, yams, cassava/yucca, quinoa, millet, amaranth, faro, bulgur, buckwheat (kasha), peas, lima beans, fava beans, hominy, rice and wild rice. Not all food-addicted/sensitive individuals are triggered by all the grains listed above, but to avoid inadvertently adding trigger foods into your life, none of these are recommended. That is not to say that a diet cannot be formulated around or with grains, but rather, those who are food addicted should avoid them entirely. Of a group of thirty food addicts who had maintained food abstinence for 5 plus years, 91% reported abstaining from sugar, and 74% of those had eliminated flour, wheat or all grains. (Tarman, 2014, p. 75-76)

In my practice, I have found that flour is the second most common addictive food substance after sugar (not including alcohol). Clients and patients often use the word 'love' and speak with nostalgia when describing foods made with flour, especially breads and/or pastas. These behaviors are signs of invoking *Romance*; another reason flour should be avoided. When clients are asked to give up bread or pasta, which are made from flour, usually consumption of some other form of grain increases, e.g., rice, potatoes, barley, etc. I suspect this is because flour is derived from similar ingredients. Flour is essentially a grain, seed, berry or kernel crushed into very tiny particles. For example, look at a grain of brown rice. I see little difference between the whole kernel when compared to brown rice flour. The texture may be changed, but the substance is the same. I use the following analogy: flour is like a pill crushed to be snorted while grain is a pill to be consumed orally. Even though time from ingestion to effect may be different, both have a similar impact on our bodies and our brains. For this reason, if we are dealing with food as a disease of substance abuse, then we must remove the substance. Period.

When eaten, grains increase blood sugar levels. The body responds by secreting insulin, which causes fat to be stored. This can lead to weight gain and obesity. Grains also have been implicated with an incidence of inflammation and fatigue for many individuals. (Davis, 2014, p. 124-125) (Perlmutter, 2013, p. 70-71) A number of my clients, once giving up grains, express experiencing a decrease in joint aches and pains, and an increase in energy within the first one or two weeks of grain-free eating.

Whole Grains vs. Refined Grains: I believe whole grains are no better for food addicts than refined grains. Let me explain. Every kernel of grain is comprised of three parts: the germ, the bran, and the endosperm. The germ contains the nutrients from which the new plant will sprout; the bran, largely made up of fiber, is the hard-outer coating which protects the kernel; while the endosperm, comprised of roughly 80% of the kernel, is the simple starch material needed for the plant's growth. The endosperm is the portion of the grain from which 'white' flour is derived. What this means is any whole grain flour contains 80% white flour. For this reason, whole grains are as unacceptable as any other grain and should be avoided. For examples, refer to the stories in this book.

The *Trigger Free Food Plans'* **protein** choices provide the appropriate grams to ensure fullness and sustenance between meals and through the night. For this reason, proteins listed may have different weighed serving amounts. To provide for the growing number of food addicts who prefer to follow a vegetarian, vegan, or pescatarian lifestyle, soy and beans and lentils have been included. These items are not required but are available. In my experience, some food addicts can eat beans and lentils while others experience an increase in cravings. If unsure, create a trial period of one month without beans and lentils to evaluate if they may be triggering you.

The *Trigger Free Food Plans* include a serving of **fruit/berries** in the morning. Fruit/berries contain natural forms of sugar which many food addicts tolerate well, while others may experience cravings. For this reason, fruits containing the highest amounts of sugar, high on the glycemic index scale, are not included. Dried fruits, as well as fruits containing added sugar are not allowed. If one experiences craving, berries, excluding strawberries, are the best option; they contain the least amount of sugar. For those who are sensitive and for those who seek flexibility, vegetables may be used to replace part or all of the fruit serving. **Note:** Because fruit is high in carbohydrates a fat is included with breakfast to help slow down the absorption of the fruit's natural sugar.

The *Trigger Free Food Plans* include a variety of **vegetables**. It is advised to consume an assortment of vegetables including both raw and cooked. In the first month, an adjustment period may be required to adapt to eating the fiber and roughage the vegetables provide, especially in the *Low Carbohydrate Plan*. Initially, some individuals will be unable to eat raw vegetables and may require only cooked. However, over time, the stomach will adjust, and raw vegetables will most likely become more tolerable. If you continue to have difficulty, consult your medical provider or your food addiction-based support/clinician. Give your taste buds a chance to change! After having eaten highly processed and carbohydrate laden foods for so long, you may have developed a strong dislike for vegetables. Give it time. There is a wide variety to choose from, with many different tastes and textures. You may be pleasantly surprised to discover you love them. I have included but limited the quantities of vegetables some may consider too starchy, e.g. winter squash, carrots, pumpkin, and parsnips. They are not required. At the same time, I have excluded all vegetables, which can be refined into starch including corn, peas, or those resembling a potato, e.g. yucca, cassava, sweet potato, yam, etc. **Note:** Each plan differs in prescribed quantities. Wheat germ, is an option only included in the *Low Carbohydrate Plan*. For many it can be a useful tool to decrease the volume of vegetables when travelling. However, it can be a trigger for some individuals. If so, avoid it entirely.

The *Trigger Free Food Plans* include **fat** at each meal to keep you full and satiated. Fat could mean the difference between needing a 'pick me up' between meals and not needing one. It is a myth that fat alone leads to weight gain. I encourage the use of the least processed oils: olive oil over vegetable oil; butter over margarine; MCT (Medium Chain Triglycerides) or coconut oil over palm oil. For this reason, I discourage the use of cooking sprays when preparing foods. They are highly processed and often contain harmful ingredients, e.g. chemicals and preservatives and may contain traces of alcohol, which is excluded from these food plans. Nuts and seeds, included to support the vegetarian, are categorized as fats because the majority of their energy comes from the oils they contain. For accuracy, I recommend weighing them. If you have an addiction to crunch or a creamy mouth feel, I suggest avoiding nuts and seeds entirely. **Note:** Each plan differs in prescribed quantities. The *High Fat Low Carbohydrate Plan* is designed to use fat as the primary energy source to produce ketones.

Water Intake: It is important *everyday,* to consume at least 64 oz. of water *throughout* the day. This does not include coffee, tea, flavored sparkling water, and sugar free and/or artificially sweetened beverages. I suggest you avoid drinking with meals as it decreases the time food spends in the stomach. This may lead to suboptimal digestion and a quicker return to perceived hunger as well as the inability to comfortably consume your entire meal. For every 30-60 minutes of moderate exercise, your fluid needs will increase by 8-12 oz. per day. **Note:** By continually consuming enough water throughout the day, gallstone formation, often triggered by rapid weight loss, can be reduced. (El-Sharkawy, Sahota, & Lobo, 2015)

Alcohol: Alcohol is not part of these food plans. It is a mind-altering substance largely composed of foods that are highly addictive. Foods that contain or are cooked/prepared with alcohol must also be avoided. Remember cooking sprays may contain alcohol. I urge my clients to avoid bars, weddings, and social engagements involving alcohol as well as their food triggers until they have sustained abstinence and sound recovery. If you decide to attend, make sure you have a good enough reason to be there. More importantly, have a planned exit strategy in place. If you experience *guilt, debate, or romance* or are considering picking up remove yourself immediately. Howl for the support of the Wolfe Pack!

Caffeine: Research has shown that caffeine is able to bypass the blood brain barrier and can affect the brain's ability to slow down. (Davis et al., 2003) Many individuals in long term food addiction recovery experience no negative consequences. However, this is not true for everyone. If you are addicted to caffeine it should be avoided completely. It should be noted that caffeine is found in diet soft drinks and cocoa powder. If you decide to give up caffeine, you may experience physical and emotional withdrawal symptoms which may include headaches, irritability, moodiness, poor focus, muscle cramps, lack of energy and/or motivation, etc.

Weight Loss: *Weight loss may be and most often will be a result of this food plan, but it **is not the primary purpose or aim**.* The purpose is to remove triggering food and sustain health and satiety for those suffering from food addiction. Each person will lose weight at a different pace. This pace can not be determined, although it is influenced by several factors including: gender, body type, starting weight, and/or ethnicity. In the beginning of eating abstinently, you may notice a large portion of weight is lost. This is common, although not always the case. **Note:** Rapid weight loss may put you at risk for the formation of gallstones. To help to avoid this, be sure to consume plenty of water throughout the day.

BEHAVIORS AND HABITS TO CONSIDER

Sleep: For weight loss, it is important to sleep at least *seven consecutive hours* in a 24-hour period. (Banks & Dinges, 2007) To ensure consistency, I encourage you to maintain the same wake up time from day to day including weekends, holidays, and vacations. Inadequate sleep may lead to a series of biochemical consequences within your body which, may increase the likelihood of you seeking your food triggers (Lustig, 2012, p. 69) and potentially losing your abstinence. In addition, I have found individuals who do shift work or work nights have more difficulty losing weight.

Exercise: When starting this plan, do not begin a new exercise program. This will be counter-productive to your recovery and goals for abstinence. Exercise creates an energy deficit, which may potentially lead to hunger and cravings. However, if you are used to a routine exercise program, there is no need to eliminate your routine. The point is, if you are a seldom/non- exerciser, now is not the time to start. I do encourage the use of cyclical and repetitive movements, early in and throughout recovery, this movement should be *meaningful not strenuous.* For example, a calm meditative walk in nature, as opposed to a high impact walk/run around the track. Other cyclical repetitive movements may have a similar positive benefit, e.g. knitting, crocheting, adult coloring books, jigsaw puzzles etc. These movements are tactile and require increased focus which can help to quiet the mind from food thoughts and cravings. Once the food plan is established, perhaps after two to three months or more, exercise can be *gradually* added. When intense exercise becomes routine, the food plan may need to be adjusted appropriately. Seek help from me or your food addiction provider. Most clinicians do not have experience working with food addicts abstaining from their, trigger foods, e.g.

sugar, flour, grains, etc. Their advice could be very harmful to you and your recovery. Prior to working with me, many of my clients had this experience and lost their abstinence. Let the Wolfe Pack help to support your abstinence.

VITAMINS AND SUPPLEMENTS

Please be aware in the U.S. the vitamin and supplement market is totally unregulated. These substances should be taken only after careful consideration and under the guidance of an informed medical provider. If you are post bariatric surgery, follow your center's guidelines and recommendations. Many vitamins on the market contain sugar. Read the ingredient list carefully; your vitamin should contain 0 calories and should not be a gummy or a soft chew.

Multivitamins are not necessary for everyone. However, if you have been taking them all along, I would encourage you to continue this practice.

B Vitamins, mostly found in grains and in a few certain meats and vegetables, will not be nutritionally provided by foods in either of the *Trigger Free Food Plans*. I encourage taking a B complex to cover all of your bases. **Note:** See *Condiments* found in *Permissible Add-Ons* of the food plan for details on nutritional yeast, which is the only vegetarian food source that provides vitamin B-12.

Vitamin D is known as the sunshine vitamin. It plays a very important role in bone health and has been related to many other health benefits. (Pludoski et al., 2013) (Holick, 2004) I encourage having your vitamin D level checked annually. If low, ask your medical provider for recommendations.

Omega-3 Fatty Acids, due to their anti inflammatory properties, are now considered a disease fighting compound. It is recommended that two servings (or 8 oz.) of cold water fatty fish be consumed weekly. (Kris-Etherton, Grieger, & Ethertonm 2009) If fish is unable to be consumed, this can be replaced by taking 1,000 mg or 1g of omega-3 fatty acids daily. Literature supports the use of up to 4g or 4,000 mg of fish oil daily without significant risk. (Mori, 2014) **Note:** The omega-3 found in flax seed does not have the same degree of health benefit as compared with fish/seafood sources, e.g. fish or krill oil.

MEDICAL CONSIDERATIONS

Diabetes: It is not uncommon for food addicts to have diabetes. These plans could lower your blood sugar drastically, and medications, especially insulin, may need to be adjusted regularly. Both low and high blood sugar levels can lead to serious consequences including death. Before starting these plans, I urge you to speak directly to your primary care provider, your diabetes clinician, and a dietitian with knowledge and experience with both diabetes and food addiction as well as low carbohydrate eating. Keeping all your providers informed is crucial. Changes in medication and/or food may need to occur frequently over a length of time to catch and/or prevent unhealthy blood sugar levels. Working together with your providers will help ensure a long-lasting healthy abstinence.

Pregnancy/Lactation: During the first trimester of pregnancy there are no changes to the food plans. Nausea is quite common. Some individuals find it easier to eat mostly cooked vegetables. Others require splitting their meals into smaller portions, while still consuming the same daily amounts. Discuss this with your food sponsor and/or medical/nutrition provider.

During the second trimester **one** metabolic (equivalent to ½ protein serving plus ½ fat serving) is added either after breakfast **or** after dinner. Typically, during this trimester nausea decreases.

During the third trimester as well as lactation a total of **two** metabolics are added. One after breakfast **and** one after dinner.

Food Plan During Pregnancy and Lactation	
Trimester	Plan Adjustments
First	No Changes
Second	1 Metabolic
Third and Lactation	2 Metabolics

Bariatric Considerations: I encourage annual nutrition/medical follow up regardless of how long it has been since your surgery. As mentioned in the vitamins and supplements section, vitamins will be an absolute necessity for those individuals who have had bariatric surgery. Comply with your center's vitamin recommendations. Also, three meals a day may not be appropriate for the size of your stomach. From my experience, most bariatric professionals who think they understand food addiction do not. This may threaten your chances for abstinence and food-based recovery. I encourage all bariatric surgery clients to work individually with a trained food addiction clinician, to create a personalized food plan.

ESSENTIAL TOOLS FOR SUCCESS

Digital Scale: I recommend everyone has at least two digital scales. One is designed to stay on your kitchen counter or in your cooking workspace. The other is designed to travel with you in your purse, backpack or car along with backup batteries. The scale for everyday use should be durable. My favorite food scale is back lit and has large numbers for easy reading. It is a workhorse and meant to take a beating from day to day use. I prefer a much smaller scale for the road. There are so many models on the market. Take a look at your options and choose according to what is most important to you. Many can be easily purchased online and/or in local hardware stores. It is not excessive to have additional option available, which might be a scale at work and/or in the car. I have heard it said, "failing to prepare is preparing to fail." **Note:** Digital scales do not always work offshore. An analog scale may be necessary.

Food Journal: Choose a journal you like. Something you will look forward to writing in everyday.

ESSENTIAL EVERYDAY PRACTICES

- Right after dinner, plan your meals for the next 24 hours.
- Write your planned meals in your Food Journal.
- Include a Daily Intention (e.g., "I will follow my food plan and be kind to others," "I will do something special for myself today," etc.) along with your food entry.
- Prepare your planned weighed and measured meals.
- Eat your meals four to six hours apart.
- Perform a Check-In at the end of the day by reviewing your Food Journal. Did you eat what you had planned? Did you accomplish your Daily Intention? If not, what can you change for the next day? It may be helpful to write down your responses and share them with someone who will understand.

Note: The *Trigger Free Food Plans* ask you to eliminate your trigger foods. Many individuals find this process is easier when done with someone else. Find a friend, family member or group with similar goals and work together. Being able to rely on one another for support will greatly enhance your ability to get and stay abstinent. Stay connected to the Wolfe Pack!

Example of a page in Food Journal including meals and Daily Intention for a woman following the Low Carbohydrate Plan

January 23rd, 2018
Breakfast:

> 2 oz Eggs
> 2 oz Feta Cheese
> ½ oz Salted butter

Lunch:

> 4 oz Chicken
> 4 oz Salad
> 8 oz Cauliflower
> 4 oz Squash
> ½ oz Olive Oil

Dinner:

> 6 oz Salmon
> 8 oz Salad
> 12 oz Spinach
> ½ oz Olive Oil
> ½ Oz Butter

Daily Intention: I will eat the foods that I commited and eat nothing in between. This is what I need to nourish and heal my body and live free from cravings. Today I will take care of myself.

Nightly Check In: Today I followed my food plan as committed and I am abstinent. 24 hours free from Guilt, Debate and Romance! I am a success!

TRIGGER FREE FOOD PLANS

Female Food Plans:

Low Carbohydrate Plan:

Breakfast:
1 Protein
1 Fruit or 8 oz. Vegetable
1 Fat

Lunch:
1 Protein
16 oz. Vegetables
1 Fat

Dinner:
1 Protein
20 oz. Vegetables
2 Fats

High Fat Low Carbohydrate Plan:

Breakfast:
1 Protein
3 oz. Berries (BBR)★
3 Fats

Lunch:
1 Protein
8 oz. Vegetables
3 Fats

Dinner
1 Protein
8 oz. Vegetables
3 Fats

Male Food Plans:

Low Carbohydrate Plan:

Breakfast:
1 Protein
1 Fruit or 12 oz. Vegetables
1 Fat

Lunch:
1.5 Proteins
16 oz. Vegetables
1 Fat

Dinner:
1.5 Proteins
20 oz. Vegetables
2 Fats

Exception List

Limit winter squash, pumpkin, carrots or parsnips to 8 oz. per day.

An optional ½ oz of unsalted seeds may be added to either lunch **or** dinner. Permissible Seeds are unsalted and may include: Sesame, flax, poppy, sunflower, chia, and squash/pumpkin.

*Blackberries, Blueberries, Raspberries

High Fat Low Carbohydrate Plan:

Breakfast:
1.5 Protein
3 oz. Berries (BBR)*
3 Fats

Lunch:
1.5 Proteins
8 oz. Vegetables
4 Fats

Dinner:
1.5 Proteins
8 oz. Vegetables
4 Fats

Exception List

In order to use fat as a primary energy source the following is recommended:

- Limit winter squash, pumpkin, carrots, and parsnips to 4 oz per day.
- Limit tomatoes to 2 oz per day including permissible add-ons.
- Avoid soy products. This plan is not intended for vegetarians or vegans.
- Avoid Cocoa

The only Fats to be used are Avocado, Coconut, and Olive Oil; Avocado; Butter; Ghee; and Animal Fat Sources. Products containing only these fats may also be used e.g., mayonnaise made with avocado oil.

FOR ALL PLANS:

(Note: Refer to *Exception Lists*)
Permissible Protein Options

Any combination of protein choices may be used if the combination equals the allotted prescription. **All proteins are to be weighed after they are cooked.**

An example for a woman's dinner might be as follows: 8 oz. of milk, which equals 2 oz. of her protein serving, so now she has 2 oz. remaining. This could easily be fulfilled with 2 oz. of poultry or meat; 3 oz. of fish; or 4 oz. of cottage cheese or yogurt.

An example for a man's dinner might be as follows: 8 oz. of milk, which equals 2 oz. of his protein serving, so now he has 4 oz. remaining. This could be easily fulfilled with 4 oz. of poultry or meat; 6 oz. of fish; or 8 oz. of cottage cheese or yogurt.

All the following are equivalent to 1 Protein choice:

Fowl/poultry 4 oz.

Pork 4 oz.

Beef 4 oz.

Game 4 oz.

Fish 6 oz.

Dried Fish 3 oz.

Shellfish 6 oz.

Eggs, 2 large or extra-large or jumbo or 4 oz.

Egg Whites/Egg Beaters 6 oz.

Milk 16 oz.

Soymilk, plain/unsweetened (grain free) 16 oz.

Kefir 16 oz.

Sour milk/European buttermilk 16 oz.

Kefir Cheese 6 oz.

Ricotta Cheese 4 oz.

Cottage Cheese 8 oz.

Hard Cheese 2 oz.

Feta Cheese 4 oz.

Goat Cheese 4 oz.

Plain Yogurt, Greek or Regular 8 oz., no sugar or grain

Skyr 8 oz.

Quark 8 oz.

Soy Cheese (no grain, no sugar) 4 oz.

Soy Flakes 4 oz.

Soy Flour, 4 oz.

Soy Grits 4 oz.

Soy Nuts 4 oz.

Soy Nut Butter 4 oz.

Soy Yogurt, plain (no sugar or grain added) 8 oz.

Texturized Vegetable or Soy Protein 4 oz.

Tofu, Extra Firm 6 oz.

Tofu, Firm, 8 oz.

Tofu, Silken or Soft 10 oz.

Tempeh, (grain free) 4 oz.

Beans, prepared: black, kidney, roman, pinto, northern, red beans, pink beans, garbanzo beans

8 oz.

Beans, roasted: black, kidney, roman, pinto, northern, red beans, pink beans, garbanzo beans

4 oz.

Lentils, cooked 8 oz.

Permissible Fresh Fruit Options

Acai berry 8 oz.

Ackee 8 oz.

Apples 8 oz. or 1 whole

Apricots (fresh) 4 each or 8 oz.

Bilberries 8 oz.

Blackberries 8 oz.

Blueberries 8 oz.

Boysenberries 8 oz.

Cantaloupe ½ each or 8 oz.

Cloudberries 8 oz.

Cherimoya 8 oz.

Clementine/Mandarin 3 each or 8 oz.

Cranberries (fresh) 8 oz.

Elderberries 8 oz.

Figs (fresh) 2 each or 8 oz.

Gooseberries 8 oz.

Grapefruit 1 piece 8 oz.

Guava 3 each or 8 oz.

Honey Dew Melon 8 oz.

Huckleberries 8 oz.

Jujubes (fruit) 8 oz.

Kiwi 3 each or 8 oz.

Kumquat 10 each or 8 oz.

Lingonberries 8 oz.

Lychees 20 each or 8 oz. peeled

Mangosteen 8 oz.

Mulberries 8 oz.

Muskmelon 8 oz.

Nectarines 8 oz.

Oranges 8 oz. or 1 whole

Papaya 8 oz.

Passion Fruit 6 each or 8 oz.

Peaches 8 oz. or 1 whole

Persimmon 4 each or 8 oz.

Pineapple 8 oz.

Plums 3 each or 8 oz.

Pluots 1 piece or 8 oz.

Prickly Pear 8 oz.

Quince 2 each or 8 oz.

Rambuton 25 each or 8 oz.

Raspberries 8 oz.

Rose Apple 4 each or 8 oz.

Sapodilla 8 oz.

Star Fruit 3 each or 8 oz.

Strawberries 8 oz.

Tangelo 2 each or 8 oz.

Tangerines 1 piece or 8 oz.

Ugli Fruit 2 each or 8 oz.

Mixed Fruit 8 oz. (any of the above)

Permissible Vegetable Options

Acorn Squash

Alfalfa Sprouts

Anise

Artichoke, Globe Artichoke

Arugula/Rockets

Asparagus

Beets

Belgian Endive

Bell Pepper

Bok Choy/Chinese Cabbage

Borage

Bottle Gourd/Calabash

Broccoli

Broccoli Rabe

Broccolini/Baby Broccoli

Brussel Sprouts

Buttercup Squash

Butterhead Lettuce

Butternut Squash/Butternut Pumpkin

Cabbage

Cabbage Sprouts

Calabaza Squash/West Indian Pumpkin

Carrot

Cauliflower

Celeriac/Celery Root

Celery

Ceylon Spinach

Chard/Silverbeet

Chayote Squash

Cherry Tomatoes

Chickweed

Chicory

Chile Peppers

Chinese Chives

Chinese Mallow

Collard Greens

Coral Lettuce

Cucumber

Daikon

Dandelion Greens

Delicata Squash

Dinosaur Kale/Lacinato Kale

Dulse

Eggplant/Aubergine

Endive

Escarole

Fennel/Finocchio

Fiddlehead Fern/Pohole

Florence Fennel

Flowering Cabbage

French Beans/Green Beans

Garden Cress

Garlic

Gem Squash

Gherkin

Ginger

Globe Eggplant

Golden Nugget Squash

Golden Samphire

Good King Henry

Green Onion/Scallion

Hakurei Turnip

Horseradish

Hubbard Squash

Ice Plant

Italian Sweet Pepper

Japanese Pumpkin/Kabocha Squash

Japanese/Chinese Eggplant

Jicama

Kai-lan/Chinese Broccoli

Kale

Kabocha Squash

Kelp

Kim chi, no sugar* or grain

Kohlrabi/German Turnip

Komatsuna

Kombu

Kurrat/Egyptian Leek

Lagos Spinach

Land Cress

Laver

Leeks

Lettuce

Lotus Root/Renkon

Mache

Malabar Spinach

Marrow Squash

Mitsuba

Mizuna

Morel/Morchella

Mulukhiyah

Mushrooms

Fungus

Mustard Greens

Mustard Spinach

Myoga

Nettles

New Zealand Spinach

Nopales

Nori

Okra

Onions

Pak Choi/Chinese Cabbage

Parsley Root

Parsnips

Pattypan Squash

Pickles (sugar free*)

Pickled Vegetables (sugar free* no olives)

Pointed Gourd

Prussian Asparagus

Pumpkin

Purslane

Radicchio

Radish

Ramps

Rhubarb

Ridge Cucumber

Ridge Gourd

Romanesco Broccoli

Rutabaga/Swedish Turnip

Salad Turnip

Samphire

Sauerkraut (sugar free*)

Scallions/Spring Onions

Sea Beet

Sea Grape

Shallots

Sierra Leone Bologi

Snake Gourd

Sorrel

Spaghetti Squash

Spinach

Spring Greens

Squash

Squash Blossoms

Tatsoi

Tinda/Apple Gourd

Tomatillo

Tomato

Turnips

Tuscan Kale

Wakame

Wasabi

Water Chestnut

Water Spinach

Watercress

Welsh Onion

White Eggplant

Winter Melon

Winter Purslane/Miner's Lettuce

Yard long Beans

Yellow Squash/Summer Squash

Yow Choy

Yu Choy Sum

Zucchini/Courgette

Only included as part of the *Low Carbohydrate* plan:

Wheat Germ (1 oz. is equivalent to 8 oz. of vegetables)

Permissible Fat Options

The following may be used as an equivalent to 1 Fat: 1 <u>level</u> Tablespoon or ½ oz. of Fat.

Butter 1 Tablespoon or ½ oz.

Margarine (grain free) 1 Tablespoon or ½ oz.

Mayonnaise (sugar free, grain free) 1 Tablespoon or ½ oz.

Vegenaise (sugar free, grain free) 1 Tablespoon or ½ oz.

Salad Dressing (sugar free, not lite or fat free) 2 Tablespoons or 1 oz.

Vegetable and Nut Oils 1 Tablespoon or ½ oz.

Olive Oil 1 Tablespoon or ½ oz.

MCT or Coconut Oil 1 Tablespoon or ½ oz.

Palm Oil 1 Tablespoon or ½ oz.

Sesame seed oil 1 Tablespoon or ½ oz.

Seed and Nut Butters (excluding Soy Nut Butter★) 2 Tablespoons

Tahini 2 Tablespoons or 1 oz.

Seeds 1 oz. – Sesame, flax, poppy, sunflower, chia, squash/pumpkin seeds

Avocado 2 oz.

Nuts, raw, **unsalted,** shelled:

Almonds 18 each or 1 oz.

Walnuts 14 halves or 1 oz.

Cashews 18 each or 1 oz.

Brazil 6 each or 1 oz.

Pecans 12 halves or 1 oz.

Pistachios 30 each or 1 oz.

Pine nuts 1 oz.

Peanuts 1 oz.

★Soy Nut Butter & Soy Nuts are listed as Protein

Permissible Add-Ons

(**Note:** Refer to *Exception Lists*)

Tomato Products: 2 oz. of tomato paste, sauce, sugar free ketchup or salsa may be used at two meals daily. Sun dried tomatoes may be used, but are double-counted, meaning 1 oz. may be consumed in place of 2 oz. of tomato product. Sun dried tomatoes should not be included as part of your vegetable serving.

Condiments: Mustard, vinegar (balsamic, red, white, cider, apple), wheat/grain free soy sauce, Bragg's Liquid Aminos ™, and lemon and lime juice may be used as free foods. Cocoa, nutritional yeast, sugar free jam and sugar free maple syrup must be limited to 2 Tablespoons per day. You may also combine them if you choose, e.g. using 1 Tablespoon sugar free maple syrup and 1 Tablespoon nutritional yeast.

ADVERSE CHILDHOOD EXPERIENCES (ACE) OR TRAUMA

To date the largest study ever done to examine the health and social effects of adverse childhood experiences included 18,000 participants. It was done in the mid-1980s by Kaiser Permanente researchers who noticed that the high dropout rate in participants in an obesity reduction program in San Diego, California was correlated with sexual abuse amongst the dropouts and the abuse occurred prior to the obesity. The outcome included 10 categories of adverse childhood experiences:

During the intervening years, researchers have continued to use this productive diagnostic tool to assess for precursors to individual, familial, community, and cultural phenomena resulting later in the lives and relationships of those interviewed.

If this were a checklist and I did not need to disclose the information on the individual items, how many of them would I check from my personal experience? (Please include this number in the trauma section on the interview question list.)

Child Maltreatment

1. Physical abuse
2. Emotional abuse
3. Sexual abuse
4. Emotional neglect
5. Physical neglect

Trauma in the household

    6. Substance abuse
    7. Mental illness
    8. Mother treated violently
    9. Imprisoned household member
  10. Loss of parent/abandonment

Other actions may be necessary to support the continuation of abstinence over time; however, abstinence from trigger foods and behaviors is the basis needed to accomplish all the other tasks. Even those who have experienced ACE, may live a blissful, contented, and productive life most days.

50 DAYS TO FREEDOM FROM CRAVINGS, CLARITY OF MIND, AND THE TOOLBOX FOR WELLBEING

Your FIX to STOP CRAVINGS

For whom? Anyone suffering from cravings and wanting to change and addicts of any ilk ready for a "do-over"

Week Three: AWARENESS

What IS reality now and What do I want to Change in Thought, Word, Deed, and Commitment? What has NOT worked previously?

Terms

1. An **addict**? Not me!

> What is an addict? A simple definition equals a "yes" to the question, "Do you have cravings?" Oh. More explanations and definitions exist: (brain chemistry, habituation, highly processed food items, process addiction vs biochemical; rats and humans.) Be truthful as you can with yourself. Has moderation worked for you? If so, with what and in what circumstances and when? Where are you now?
>
> One woman described her state as "Sad, obese, out of control, unfocused, and depressed again.": Her goal was

to be under 200 pounds and on her way again to her size 14 clothing again. Courage and self-control were her aspirations. What are your specific goals for these 7 weeks and one day? William Glasser suggested decades ago that if we want change, substitution is necessary. "We need to fulfill basic needs: the need to love and be loved and the need that we are wortwhile to ourselves and others." He asked "What are you going do about your life, beginning today."

https://www.latimes.com/local/obituaries/la-me-william-glasser-20130828-story.html

2. **Change:** something you want to do, feel, or have (or do, have or be) which is different from what you do, feel, or have now

TO DO

- Eat abundantly
- Laugh and play
- Sleep restfully and peacefully
- Travel in planes comfortably in one seat without an extension
- Prepare healthy, delicious meals inexpensively and efficiently
- Clear clutter from the mind, physical environment, and body
- Release excess weight, food, possessions
- Release procrastination and excesses of all kinds: real and perceived
- Laugh out loud with grandchildren and friends
- Share memory-making with friends and relatives
- Think clearly free from a head filled with brain fog or mashed potatoes
- Without fatigue doing what's on your bucket list
- Walking enthusiastically without the pain of aching joints
- Giving, sharing, experiencing life as you once did
- Enjoying smaller and unimaginably maybe even single-digit clothing sizes
- Breathing consciously and freely without a CPAP machine

TO HAVE

- Freedom to wear a swimsuit or ski or Jazzercise
- Relationships without eggshell walking
- Contentment playing on the floor with children and grandchildren
- Relationships based on integrity and responsibility for self not the other
- Wisdom to put on my own oxygen mask first and help others and respond to their needs only to the extent I do no harm to myself
- Ability to create boundaries clear enough to contain myself as I grow and change and to keep others from impinging on my newfound choices
- A sense of well-being in body, mind, and spirit
- A space between thought and action
- Energy to accomplish plans and attain goals
- Time to fulfill dreams unrealized
- Relationships based on honesty and shared aspirations
- Abundance of resources to do what is desired
- Intuition to access and experience what is enough (food, material possessions, memory, the capacity to love, money with which to be altruistic, relationships that nurture and support and enhance, and creativity to generate positivity: the best me in relation with you)

TO BE/TO FEEL

- Content
- Free from cravings
- Mindful
- Meditating on joyful possibilities
- Peaceful
- Compassionate
- Kind to self and others
- Living what you could only dream before
- Creative enough to write, paint, photograph, sculpt, direct....
- Expressing love freely

- Being the person you always longed to be
- Generous
- Risk-taking
- Altruistic and purposeful
- At ease in your own skin
- No longer fleeing responsibility or individuation
- Seeking maturity and wisdom
- A new enthusiasm for life
- Delighting in rainbows in Hawaii (or anywhere else)
- Soaking away tension in Icelandic blue waters (or in your own bubble bath)
- Wading in turquoise water with white sand between your toes
- Giggling with grandchildren playing with unicorns and fairy dust
- Fill in your own blank!

3. **FIX**: a change that moves you in the direction you wish to go!

- ★ Might be a substance or change of substance
- ★ A behavior change (added or subtracted)
- ★ Acceptance of a continuation for x days or time period to experience the desired effects
- ★ PLUS the decision to continue or change in a new way

What are the tools I have acquired this week for my toolbox?

Homework: What are the SMARTEST goals this week:

1. Food
2. Another behaviour

   Prepare your goals and write them and your responses in your journal.

Week Four: ABSTINENCE

what is abstinence and what is it Not? What do I know and need to learn about what in order to be successful to choose abstinence? To do, have, be/ feel all that is described above

Am I an addict?

What is an addiction?

Biochemical

How does it feel in my body?

Rat research/Nicole Avena; check her out!

How could abstinence be the solution?

Have I tried everything else?

Have I tried abstinence before? With what results? And for how long?

Quote from **Alcoholics Anonymous**: "The only solution we have to offer is complete abstinence." (It has worked for millions of alcoholics for 85 years. Might it work for you? What have you got to lose?)

Isn't that too hard a solution?

It may be the easiest solution you've ever tried.

Have I already failed the course?

You're invited to use abstinence and be part of the A-team. Try it! You can howl with the Wolfe Pack too!

What are the next steps?

Homework: Prepare:

- What do I crave? List what comes to mind immediately.
- Be curious and honest with yourself.
- What am I willing to change and for what reasons?
- How serious am I about making this change?
- Write down three days of what foods, beverages, and snacks you eat and drink plus the number of hours you sleep and times slept plus the exercise/movement you do: what and how much and how long
- Do something to celebrate your successes! Notice and acknowledge them. This is one day at a time, not necessarily for the rest of your life: today. Many choose to eliminate sugar. If that has not worked in the past, you may find grains: pasta, bread, and alcohol may be the problem. You may commit to what you are willing to do. All of that works. For some withdrawal one time may be an easier path than piecemeal withdrawal or the Weaning off method.

Prepare your SMARTEST goals and write them and your responses in your journal.

Week Five: ACTIONS

What body/gut changes do I need? What am I willing to do?

Cleaning out the kitchen

Requesting support from a buddy or accountability partner and making daily commitments

Sleep: and water: how much do I need to be healthy really?!

What mindfulness processes will support my mind and spirit, brain and emotions

Boundaries for tantrums and traumas?

Technology toys and facts: what addictions (or if not addictions the verbal wars inside me) do I experience?

Values what do I really, really, really want my life to be and how does what I eat or abstain from eating help or harm me?

Practicing what supports my self-chosen abstinences and well-being: could this really give me my dreams?

An emphatic YES, most say who have tried this process and have stuck with the A-team! Abstinence.

Commitments

Turn over the house

Remove those substances from which you plan to abstain

Bring in from the market items that do not include any in your homework list below

As William James said: "Begin flamboyantly!"

Just one day at a time

Homework: What unprocessed foods can I choose and purchase? SEE DAVE AVRAM'S TWO EATING PLANS and CHOOSE ONE. So many choices. make your choice and stick to it today.

Prepare your SMARTEST goals and write them and your responses in your journal.

Week Six: ACCOUNTABILITY

Boundaries to help or are they a hindrance in creating a new life?

Promises kept will/won't: just for today no matter what! No exceptions!

How do I hold myself accountable to my new commitments?

What changes do I need to make to support abstinence?

Who are the people who support me and what I want to accomplish?

When and how I'd invite them to do so?

Some people choose to join groups (twelve-step groups or church-related groups specific to your need)

Some people choose to create groups (*The Artist's Way* by Julia Cameron or The Fix by Cynthia Myers Morrison and Dave Wolfe) or mastermind groups

The real Economics is a relationship too: how do I spend my time and money and energy?

(If I had $500, what would I do with it?) Or how do I want to change my spending of time and money?

Allocations and altruism: how much and how do I choose to share my time, talents, and treasures to support others (family, friends, work, organizations, and myself?)

What support and how much and how often do I need to receive it and give it?

Commitments

Write out your commitment to abstinence **from what** *for how long*.

Share your commitment with another. Choose SMARTEST goal setting patterns.

Homework

Answer the questions above and review your answers with a person in a group or someone you trust.

Attend one twelve-step group for food or create a group of your own if you have not yet done so. This is easier with compatriots.

Do something to celebrate your successes!

Week Seven: ACCEPTANCE

Myself, Others, My choices, Commitments, Change Process, and Abstinence is the Solution

How do I accept myself as I am?

How do I accept myself when I am becoming something else?

How do I accept others as they are?

Even when they may be sabotaging my abstinence purposefully or by mistake?

How do I accept my choices positive and negative?

How do I turn over mistakes? And then forgive myself for them?

How do I expect less than perfection while striving for a perfect abstinence?

Prepare your SMARTEST goals and write them and your responses in your journal.

Commitments

To hold steadfast my commitments to my accountability partner and abstinence **no matter what** (under any and all conditions).

How do I hold my commitments sacred, as though I held my agreements with my accountability partner and the universe in a sacred space?

Homework: How do I accept the difficulties of the change process?

How do I accept the successes of the change process? Including potentially substantial weight loss and all that that brings?

Since abstinence is the solution for cravings, how do I live in the New World so different from the one I lived in so recently?

Week Eight: APPRECIATION

Gratitude for abstinence No Matter What!

Some members of twelve-step groups greet each other with the response to "How are you?": "Abstinent and grateful!" This is perceived to be true independent of anything else that's going on in one's life!

In what ways might I express this appreciation?

What relationships current and past have sustained me through hard times and in good times?

What gifts of spirit, material possessions, emotional offerings etc. have I received without gratitude or without thanks expressed to the one who gifted me? How might I redress these now?

How does gratitude change relationships?

Is money required in order to express appreciation?

How does timing influence appreciation granted and received?

Might I practice appreciation with everyone with whom I interact in a particular hour or day or place?

Prepare your SMARTEST goals and write them and your responses in your journal.

Commitments: I am grateful!

Homework: For what am I grateful?

Body, mind, spirit, relationships, interactions with colleagues, socialization, commitments, finance, energy, health, bliss, contentment, productivity, and hopefullness.

Week Nine: ASSESSMENT

What has worked and what has not? Where to go from here? Body, Mind, Spirit, Emotions, Social, Career, Financial?

Abstinence and what comes next?

Detox past? Or another detox to let go of one more substance or behavior?

Then with time, what has abstinence given and taken away?

What freedom, choices, strategies do I need today?

The A-team supports 100 percent Abstinence From What Harms Me.

That may change over time.

Aging and gravity.

Prepare your SMARTEST goals and write them and your responses in your journal.

Commitments: Do something to celebrate your successes!

Homework: ongoing implementation

Grocery shopping

Planning, preparing, protecting, pausing

Choosing where I eat

Choosing with whom I eat and what I eat and all the behaviors I choose

Identifying what works for me

How can I make all of these things more efficient and more comfortable and more automatic; like flossing and brushing my teeth! Or cutting the plastic on bottles to save the otter? Or taking out the garbage in two bins: trash or recycling?

Week Ten: "A GAIN"

(discarded weight?): what awareness do I now have about which I was previously unaware? Next steps

What new abstinence in addition to continuing my current abstinence do I choose?

Some speak of spirals: when one reaches the end of a spiral, the beginning of the next is just at hand! Share your answers with another and invite their suggestions.

Recommitting

What to do when I make a mistake?

How to refrain from shame and blame?

Where to go to turn over a mistake?

What are the differences among mistakes, decisions to break an abstinence, or binges?

What constitutes success or failure? Thomas Edison

What kind of thinking has gotten me into difficulties? How can I refrain from that thinking or put that on my abstinence list as well?

Homework: Recommitting when I have wavered

Answer the questions above

Share the responses with another

Invite their sharing as well; you might be surprised!

Prepare your SMARTEST goals and write them and your responses in your journal.

Identify at least one new commitment to abstinence from a substance or behavior or abstinence to permit new behaviors (creativity, mindfullness, meditation, early to bed or?)

Commitments: continue to celebrate successes and express gratitude and appreciation at the same time as committing to new and continued abstinence with the A-Team

BONUS Automatic Negative Thoughts (ANTs) and Other Annoyances and Aggravations: Families, Friends, and Frenemies, Traumas and traumas

Relationships

Timing

Quantity

Mind chatter

What is enough?

HALT (hungry, angry, lonely, tired and sometimes serious and fabulous)

When everything is going well

When everything is going badly

What next

Prepare your SMARTEST goals and write them and your responses in your journal.

Commitments! Do something to celebrate your successes!

Homework: challenges I experience

Identifying challenges

Identifying solutions

Identifying alternatives that work

What does asking for help mean to me?

How can I acquire more support to attain my goals?

Share

Do something to celebrate your successes!

BONUS ACCIDENTS: mistakes and other imperfections! How to use accountability partners to let go of these and maintain abstinence **no matter what**

How might I assess accidents and mistakes and other imperfections? In what ways can I turn these over to my accountability partners and have them received with grace and kindness and for my partner to say, "Let it go."

How might I accept this forgiveness of a mistake or other imperfection instead of battering myself with guilt and shame and continued bingeing or starving?

How might I strive for integration instead of rigidity or chaos? (See Dr. Dan Siegel - UCLA Mindfullness Clinic)

How might I mindfully accept my humanity with all its imperfections while striving for the perfect goal of abstinence?

Prepare your SMARTEST goals and write them and your responses in your journal.

BONUS ADJUSTMENTS: and what to do to increase clarity and growth each day?

Might this include visits and potentially commitment to twelve-step program(s)?

Might this include enhanced accountability partner agreements?

Might this include new recipes for success with abstinence daily?

In what ways might preparing, planning and protecting abstinence be increased daily?

If I am successful and then waiver, what do I need to do immediately?

How might gratitude be enhanced daily?

How might celebrations be included to enhance abstinence?

Celebrations

What have I experienced with abstinence?

What has worked?

What has not worked?

What can I celebrate?

What next steps do I need to continue?

How do A-team members stay in contact to gain support and to support each other?

BONUS What to do in restaurants? Or when traveling? Or in special circumstances like being sick, having migraines, a colonoscopy, hormone challenges, visiting at mealtime in restaurants and in homes? See our blogs on sites: https://lightofcindy.wordpress.com/ and https://www.triggerfreenutrition.com/

Bonus: fun without food as the focus! List:

Bonus: Facebook group

Bonus: participation in the next book launch

Let us celebrate **our** successes!

The FIX is Fun, Informative and Xtra-ordinary Support as you clarify present and future changes and growth. Adding to your FIX continues daily, every day, one day at a time. When something does not go as planned, each person can identify new strategies to support self and to gain support in continuing with a more successful plan. Remember Thomas Edison. He may have been addicted to persistence and perseverance. It worked. We can be blissful, contented, and productive while ABSTINENT from trigger foods and behaviours. We can persist, persevere, and achieve the FIX we have always wanted.

Please stay in touch and share your victories! And feel free to post your questions at our blog sites. For more info and strategies, additional classes and groups are available to join. You are welcome to gain support to attain freedom from craving for trigger foods and behaviors.

https://lightofcindy.wordpress.com/ and https://www.triggerfreenutrition.com/

If all else fails, working with another to share your toolbox and skills will potentially save you and the others.

In this section, you will find stories of other individuals who have experienced an addiction or in many cases multiple addictions. Some may call them "substance use disorders" or may use other nomenclature. Whatever the terminology choice you prefer, please transpose the individual's term with the one you prefer. Their solutions are sometimes specific and clearly stated or they may be sometimes more generally described, as each one of us identifies the process which works in an individual case.

Without exception and simply, the solutions involve taking actions to **abstain from trigger foods and behaviors, asking for support, and then being willing to receive the support when it is offered. Another set of solutions includes taking personal responsibility for planning, preparing, and protecting abstinence and for pausing whenever out of sorts or off the beam, and for abstaining from trigger foods NO Matter What, When, Where, or Who!**

For more than three decades I worked in the field of education in many different capacities. I may always be an educator at my core. Maymie Porter, a woman I never met, influenced my life. Regularly quoted by Dr. Sidney B. Simon, a famed educator in Values Clarification, Maymie was a master teacher who asked each of her students after completion of an observation the following three questions:

1. What did you like about the lesson? You would do these things again.
2. What would you change about the lesson if you were to do it again?
3. What additional resources do you need?

What she was applying to classroom experiences, I would suggest pertinent for all of us. Might I apply them to my life today?

The question about additional resources allows me to evaluate the possibilities for change and what support and encouragement might be helpful to me individually. I am not alone. When in my hopelessness at times in my life, I thought I was alone, it was never true. "Alone" and "without resources" are 'lies' I told myself. Those kinds of words and phrases are 'scary stories' meant to amuse but I came to believe them.

Have you done the same?

Please enjoy the individuals who share their personal and often painful stories in the following section. These all have happy "endings." Yours can likewise be, if you take the actions and risks to change what doesn't work, now. Many are late stage food addicts who did not succeed earlier. May their stories inspire you? A successful sculptor and jeweler named Smokey Newton in 1971 recounted his experience of seeing a log next to his driveway. He spoke to BG (Big Girl) who he saw reclining in the wood. He removed all that was unnecessary to release the art she became. We do the same. So much of who we think we 'are' may be in fact extraneous material associated with someone else and another's beliefs, experiences, and feelings. By eliminating that which doesn't work, we can see **who and what we really are. We can be free to become who we are or to become the one we aspire to be, to do what we passionately wish to accomplish, and to have the blissful, contented, and productive life each of us chooses.**

STORIES TO INSPIRE CHANGE
NOW USING ABSTINENCE

THE STORY OF MY DISEASE

I am 65 years old, and I was overeating from when I was 11 (and I was sent to the doctor for the first time because of obesity) and continued until ten years ago. I still do not consider my illness cured, and I daily take great care with my meals.

During my life, I've tried any diet and any program that gave me some hope to stop overeating and get to a normal weight. At that time, I thought it was only about body weight, nothing else. I just wanted to be healthy and happy as any other human being does. None of the diets and programs I tried worked for more than a year. Due to these activities, I've lost at least 200 kilos in my life but got back up to 210 kilos. (Note: a kilo is 2.20462 pounds or here 463 pounds.)

Ten years ago, I was 105 kilos (Note a kilo is 2.2 pounds or here 231 pounds) at the height of 159 cm. (Note a cm is .3937 inch or here 5'2".) This by the grace of God and support of other overeaters, I've lost 47 kilos (103.4 pounds), but I also learned and accepted I have a severe disease, which can easily kill me. I believe something in my body doesn't work as it does in normal people. Some tiny mechanism or chemistry which regulates the feeling of hunger has broken. Honestly, I am a food addict, addicted to sugar and carbs.

Addiction developed during my life when I used food to comfort my feelings of anxiety, fear, loneliness, and emptiness. Sugar and carbs were my drugs of choice because I've been actively rejecting any other substance, such as nicotine, alcohol, pills, drugs, or anything similar. On the other hand, I didn't know how and couldn't share my feelings and problems in more appropriate and less harmful ways. Does addiction go with a specific personality structure? Is it given, in part, at birth?

I started abusing food in this way. I took something sweet or just tasty anytime when I felt uncomfortable. It was often due to my life circumstances. Over time the amount of food needed to feel better became bigger and bigger, but the relief failed to come. I couldn't stop eating until everything was eaten, but I still wanted more. My life had become unmanageable, and I was just waiting to die because I did not have any hope of controlling my life again. There was no way to comfort my pain.

I believe overeating is a severe disease, which is never cured and is hard to arrest as everybody must eat to survive. I've been abstaining from eating any man-made sugars, carbs, and starches for almost ten years. The craving for sugar still appears sometimes, and always I must be aware if I take in just a little, I'll be back overeating. I've experienced that many times during my attempts to lose weight and be normal. I will never be normal. I am different, and I must live with that. This disease is not only about body mass, but it's also much more: it's about feelings, relationships, a sense of life, and an experience of my place in the universe.

Many times, I've asked myself what could protect other people or me from this disease. Sometimes I feel like everyone has something, some trouble in life. This is a task to find solutions and personally grow or disintegrate. At other times, I think we have many possibilities, more guidance, and increased support to become more able to deal with life's troubles. Knowledge and social skills and abstinence protect against this and other diseases.

M.

MY FIRST "PUSHER"

My first "pusher" was my grandmother. My mother was in a mental hospital after my birth. It was the early 1940's, and sugar rationing having just been lifted, dear Granny would wrap sugar in little gauze bags and tie them with string. Walla, the Sugar Titt was born. Pacifiers weren't invented yet, and I became a 'sugarholic' from infancy. The message through childhood was always, "Don't cry; don't feel bad; here have something sweet."

By 17 yrs. of age I weighed 180 lbs., so I got married. That would fix my pain. NOT! Now free from parental authority, I ran to all my binge foods. "Don't feel, don't bother us, you don't count nor matter, swallow your feelings," became my lifetime mantra. Within a couple months I was over 200 lbs. and soon to top 270 lbs.

By the age of 33, after tons of diets, shots, and starving, I was still gaining. In 1976 I heard the term 'food addict' and I knew in my soul that this is what I had become. I entered recovery with a determination to never be fat again. I really believed getting thin would solve all life's problems. Ha, wrong! I removed immediately all trigger foods and stayed on a food plan which eliminated sugars and grains, my drugs.

I had no idea I would enter a life where all my thinking and behaviors would have to change. I have spent the last 42 years in 12 Step recovery and have maintained a healthy body weight. Life's new knowledge and a spiritual focus altered me drastically. I am filled with a joy of living. I do not touch processed sugars or grains in any form for the simple reason that sugar makes me crazy and flour makes me lazy. I seek healthy joyful foods that are life giving. I write, pray, meditate, go to 12 Step meetings, and give the gift away every day, for I know now, "Joy is the most infallible sign of the presence of God/Spirit"-- not sugar.

D.

MY ABSTINENCE DATE IS OCTOBER 14, 2009

I weighed 171.2 pounds wearing a size 14-16. I couldn't stop eating and the more I ate the more I wanted. I loved processed food: quick and easy. I craved sugar and carbohydrates. I would be watching T.V. and a commercial with food would come on and whether I was hungry or not, I had to have it. I would get in my car and drive to the first 7-11. I was stuffing my face and before I got back home, all of it was gone. I am an addict with food. I would hide food from my children or lock myself in my bedroom, so I could eat as much as I wanted.

My job would provide breakfast snacks or celebrations. I would be so embarrassed because I kept coming back for more. I would go to lunch or dinner with a co-worker, and we would share an appetizer. I would eat the whole thing. I didn't want to do this, but the compulsion for more was uncontrollable. I was on every diet every week: a weight loss program, hypnosis, diet medicine, B-12 shots, gyms, and hundreds of dollars spent on exercise equipment for my home. I always thought one day I would lose weight, and I was going to use the equipment but instead I used it to hang clothes. I was fuzzy headed, irritable, and a controller; I knew what was best for everyone. I was a people pleaser and believed once I was thin, my world would be perfect.

I was also addicted to trying diets and spreading the word that this diet was the cure. It might have been the cure but when I tried these diets, I manipulated the program to fit my needs, so they never worked for me. I had to buy everything, including "the extras" that came with the program. I would feel waves of pleasure because this was the cure for my compulsive eating. Nothing worked, I felt like a failure again, and then I just became resigned to remaining fat.

I finally found my cure. The food plan I am doing is a gift from God. I weigh 110.5 lbs. I wear between 0-2 petite in clothes at 4'11". Friends and family think I am too small. My entire life I wanted to be the weight that I am at 66 years old. It took me 60 years to find this food plan. My program is free. The biggest gift of this food plan is no food craving for foods I don't eat. That is the miracle for me. I can cook, look at it, and say, "This is not my food" or "This looks good."

I keep my eyes on my own plate, and my food is so delicious I lick the plate. Yummy. I am clear headed, and I make different decisions with my life. Food is not the answer to my problems today I sit with my feelings, and sometimes they are unbearable. Feelings are not facts and they do pass as I weigh and measure my food without exception. I have a community I can share with, and I receive excellent advice on food and life situations.

MY STORY

I was going to a food coach I paid for every week; I exercised at a high-priced gym; I had a food plan and weighed every week. I lost the same 10 lbs. for 4 months. I am a liar when it comes to food. I want what I want, and I always want it NOW. I would talk to the food coach about God.

One day she told me about a program that worked when she lived in Los Angeles. She gave me a phone number to a phone bridge. I signed up for a yahoo email group, but it took about 3 months for me to call that number. I kept hearing this slogan, 'No Matter What.' I was intrigued, and I read the emails, and something told me to stop paying this food coach money I didn't have.

My journey began. I had a lot of trouble following this food plan. I thought I was entitled to drink and eat the foods that made me feel good temporarily, especially if you had my life, troubles, work, family, and coworkers. Hell, I thought I had the right to eat any and everything as much as I wanted. Gluttony!

In this group, I heard the problems other people had and despite those, they continued to weigh and measure without exception over death, divorce, cancer, financial situations, and loss of jobs.

Today I can face life's problems without a substance or food to take away the pain. I can live life on life's terms, without exceptions. This is a hard one for this addict. I don't have to be ashamed about how I eat in front of others, a miracle. My food is to die for. The weight loss is important to me, and I wear the same size clothes year after year. My food plan is free. I am also thankful I don't have to try another fad diet I know

I can't follow because I am addicted to sugar and grains. I am willing and grateful to follow this food plan that has saved my life spiritually, emotionally, and physically.

I want to set an example for friends and family. If I can do this anyone can. I am not special. I can enjoy family affairs or celebrations without food. I am present.

My eyes are broken when it comes to food. That is why I weigh and measure without exception. It is just the right amount. This food plan gives me peace around the food. I don't have to think about New Year's and starting a new diet on Monday or "I will start this diet tomorrow."

I have a person I call who keeps me accountable. I have a community, Facebook, live meetings phone meetings, google plus, and Skype: people all over the world who weigh and measure without exception. I have friends I have never met who can share their courage, strength, and hope. I have people in my life who can show me a different way.

It doesn't have to be my way, which normally makes no sense. I am a black and white person. I am learning to have a grey area in my thinking. It is okay to be wrong. I am no different than anyone else. We all have the same problems. I don't have to isolate. I can pick up the phone anytime, and a friendly voice is on the other end to help me. I have a program that helps me live life between my meals. I use the tools daily: meditating, praying, making outreach calls, and doing service for the next food addict. This helps me keep my abstinence. I am becoming an adult at 66 years of age. All I do is weigh and measure my food without exception and do the next right thing. I am not willing every day, and sometimes I pray for willingness. I am abstinent and very grateful for this food plan. I am one of the lucky ones. God is doing for me what I cannot do for myself. I have weighed and measured my food through deaths, job loss of my husband, family crisis, vacations, and day trips. This is how: I pray, plan, and protect my food plan. I don't take anything for granted. I also weigh my own food because I am responsible for what I put in my mouth. Thank you, God.

MY FOOD ADDICTION STORY

I remember as a child desiring to eat a lot of sugary treats, ice-cream bars, candies, and bags of store-bought cookies always available in the kitchen cupboard. My mother preferred to bake pastries rather than cooking meals which she disliked, and so we did not eat nourishing meals. Canned vegetables, boiled potatoes, and some meat, frozen fish sticks or TV dinners, and canned spam were staples. I drank a lot of milk, and it was good milk, delivered in glass bottles by a milkman, and there were no antibiotics at that time in the milk. We did not have a garden, nor any fresh fruit, except watermelon in the summer or bananas. I didn't like salads, which seemed tasteless to me-- iceberg lettuce, raw onions, and maybe a pale tomato, nor did I like the bottled dressing always on the table. We ate Wonder Bread, marshmallow fluff, peanut butter, baloney sandwiches, and sometimes tuna fish sandwiches. In my lunches my mother packed for school was always a cupcake or cookies, and a baloney on white bread sandwich.

I don't mean to be critical of my mother, who was a heavy smoker and looking back, appeared to have been addicted to junk-food herself and disinterested in healthy eating. I now think that if I had had decent nutrition as a child I might not have become addicted to alcohol as a teenager.

I always thought she made the very best chocolate chip cookies to be had. Later when I worked as a teenage nanny, living with more affluent people, I was educated on how to eat healthier, but by then I had already started drinking and smoking cigarettes, and stayed on that trajectory for 10 years, until I entered recovery from alcoholism when I was 26.

At that point I had not been eating well at all for a while, and my body was malnourished. I had to learn how to take care of myself in recovery, and I learned to eat better, but I also went back to consuming a lot of sugar. A few years later in recovery, I learned about cooking more rarified and gourmet food.

There were a few years in my thirties when I thought about a career in the food industry. Becoming enamored with gourmet food, I took cooking classes, became an apprentice at a school in NYC that taught classes in all types of cuisines. I was able to attend for free, because I was the "kitchen assistant" in each class and had to do most of the cleaning up while attending the class. Later I took a couple of semesters at a technical college in Hotel and Restaurant Management, while simultaneously worked at a restaurant in their Executive Dining Room as a waitperson. I soon became a baker for one of the in-store restaurants and The Cellar department, which sold some of the items I baked in the Executive Dining kitchen after my shift as waitperson ended each day.

I did not finally pursue a food career, but I continued with my romantic idea of gourmet eating. When my husband I left New York to move out to a rural area, I enthusiastically took up vegetable gardening with the idea of living a more sustainable lifestyle. Up to this time, I was considered a thin person, and even as a child, was called names by others like, "Skinny-Minnie, or "Bones" and felt embarrassed by my thin body. It seemed I was the last person in my class to enter puberty and had to beg my mother to buy me a bra. When I was in my teens, and twenties, though, I enjoyed plenty of compliments on my figure, and kept a lovely figure until my early forties, even with all the attention I was paying to gourmet food.

When I went into recovery for alcoholism in my late twenties, I went back to eating sugary things at a low-level, in a maintenance-type manner, having bits of sugar all through the day, and I did not gain weight. I had no recognition I was in the throes of another addiction. The consequences did show up in having gum disease and having serious teeth problems, resulting in many root-canals, all of which subsequently failed.

When I reached menopause, and for me that was early--at age 43. I started to put weight on. Twenty pounds or more a decade--until in my late fifties, I was miserable about my weight. I am fairly tall so even though I noticed the gradual creeping up of my weight, I deluded myself into thinking I would surely be able to regain my lovely figure if I went on the right diet for a while, or if I exercised enough to balance out the calories I was consuming. But the gaining continued, and I became angrier and angrier about it.

I met a woman who had lost 100 lbs. through a 12-step fellowship and program, called GreySheeters Anonymous. We became friends, and I spent a lot of time with her, as she hired me at one point to do office work in her home. I ate many meals she offered based on the program she was doing, but I couldn't make the leap. Could this be a solution for me?

Instead I tried to lose weight through weight loss program, as some of my friends near my town were enthusiastic about going as a group, and for a while it seemed to work. I did lose 25 lbs., and felt better, but even with a weight loss, there was a constant obsession with food, thinking about how much I could have and focusing on snacks I was allowed. The group meetings seemed to focus a lot on how to craft fat-laden and sugar-laden desserts into a recognizable, but lower-calorie version, and they bored me, as I was hoping to learn about good nutrition.

Both my mother and my younger sister had passed away from cancer, and it seemed there might be a strong connection with their lifestyles— smoking, poor nutrition—active alcoholism in the case of my sister— and their illnesses. So, I wanted to be healthier—and yet I still wanted to be able to eat sweets. I thought if I ate only organic vegetables and fruit I might be able to work into my life the treats that had been a staple for me since I was a child. Unfortunately, that grand bargain failed me.

One day at work, there was a holiday food fest with team members bringing in all their favorite holiday foods, and a conference room was set up with breakfast with all kinds of high-carbohydrate and fat-laden foods and then again, for lunch.

A gift of insight happened for me that day. I realized I was obsessed with the food in that room, and I wanted to partake of everything; however, I didn't want people to see the amount I wanted to take, nor the compulsion to try everything. I tried to lie to myself, thinking I could take some home for my husband, and he would be pleased with all the treats. But I knew they were really for me, not for him. I also saw I had shame around my obsession.

That day I called the woman with the 100-lb weight loss who was active in _A and said I was ready to "Do GreySheet", but could I wait until after the Holidays? She laughed and said I might not be motivated after the holidays. She said I was motivated right now, and she could help me right now. And so, I began my _A journey.

In this program, I have maintained a 40-lb weight loss now for 10 years, with complete abstinence from sugars and grains, and eating weighted and measured meals from the GreySheet list of foods we can choose from and eating three meals a day with no snacking in between. This beautiful discipline has given me many gifts. I do not fight with myself around food anymore. My body has responded gratefully to better health, with less anxiety. I am sure the constant sugar ingestion fueled higher anxiety. I have better dental health, fewer colds and flus, excellent numbers in my blood work, and a stable weight which rarely fluctuates. (We weigh ourselves only once a month.)

Due to my commitment to this program, with the help of a sponsor, I also sponsor others who have experienced many of the same benefits and are as grateful as I am to have found a solution to a life-long struggle with sugar addiction. I want to stay here in the _A program, especially as I have reached my seventies, as it surely will help me keep my healthy body in a good state, and I can also be useful to others in their quests for better health.

TRAUMA

When I heard a prominent obesity expert say that for people with eating disorders, if they were to resolve the traumas which instantiated their behaviors, they would be able to eat normally, I was thrilled at the prospect.

Then I recalled the photo of me with my hands in the fudge pan and my face covered with the gooey brown sweet, and I was 18 months old. I reconsidered the possibility of normalcy. (The photo was a black-and-white photo. The brown fudge color is from years of personal experience with my favorite kind of fudge.)

There are researchers who might suggest I had already been traumatized by my mother's absence from my immediate proximity in the first six weeks of my life while my grandmother cared for me. My mother reports she was ill with flu when she returned from the hospital after my birth. My maternal grandmother then told my mother, "This is your daughter. You get out of that bed and take care of her." (My mother denies this now, but it is a story she reported earlier when her memory was less impaired. The time elapsed between my birth and my grandmother's statement may be a mistaken recollection of mine. Now I have no way of verifying without seeking railroad reservations. It could be done.)

After my grandmother's departure, my mother experienced in the first six months of my life a severe case of tonsillitis. This was just post World War II, and hospitals did not yet have supplies of penicillin. Instead of antibiotic treatment, her tonsils were lanced, and she reported lying in a darkened room at the hospital, believing she was going to die. She had given me to the neighbor in the Quonset hut area where we lived with two wood-burning stoves in three rooms. My father and mother were both students at a state college. My father was there with the benefits he had gained from service in the Army Air Corps as a pilot.

If one were to look at this set of experiences, one might note that my father had already had a potential death experience as his airplane was shot up by an enemy off the coast of Florida. He got back to the airfield and was told to land the plane and leave it at the far end of the runway. The next day he returned to see the plane in daylight. He was asked, "What plane?" (I learned these details, perhaps 50 years later.) Was he impacted by this experience, and if so, was that passed on to his daughter and wife?

My father's dyslexia may have been an irritating and humbling experience for him as it riddled his life with challenges others might not have encountered. My father spoke about his difficulties learning Morse code and his delayed graduation from flight school as the result. What stamina it must've taken to learn and process Morse code when one experienced dyslexia! (Those days delayed later changed his career path.)

At 18 months of age (the time of the fudge photo), my mother was away at college and I had been deposited with my maternal grandparents for the duration of a six-week requirement that Mother live in a home economics house to complete her graduation requirements. (The rules were changed the subsequent year, but my mother had by then graduated.) I had been toilet trained prior to her departure but regressed. My grandmother then took over the responsibility. (To the image of her long red lacquered fingernails and wagging finger in my face, I reacted with rage even as a 24-year-old, newly sober and clean. I did not want people to tell me what to do! Or what not to do?)

At age 7 we lived across the street from my mother's best friend and her husband and children. The cover story for years was "I was molested as a child." My recollections of childhood excluded that information until I was in my 20s, had a flashback/abreaction in a situation similar perhaps to what I had experienced as a child. What I recollected initially were body sensations, feelings of powerlessness and terror, and the awareness

I had some repetitive behaviors: odd even to me. My voice when distressed in any way would seem choked as though the circumference of my throat had diminished. I am right-hand dominant but probably left foot and left eye dominant. The callous on my middle finger due to the extraordinary pressure placed on it while learning to write and subsequent writing made me question if I were in fact left-handed initially and stressed in the transition. My left wrist with anything tight around it made me feel as though I were choking. I could not tolerate having a radio behind me. (When they put speakers in the rear windows of cars, my next car had to have the speakers disabled for me to be comfortable driving.) If someone massaged my shoulders, I was available sexually to them, whether I knew them or not. I would cry when I was angry. I would laugh when I was afraid. I found myself repeatedly in sexual circumstances to which I did not recall giving permission. I had what I called "brown outs" in which I remembered the beginning and the end of an experience; however, the middle was vague and without detail. I experienced physical pain as pleasure. I was fascinated with nipples and pain related to a film I had seen which was inappropriate for a child. I had a recurring dream as a child I was in the house with my childhood friend, and a giant bear outside tried to get into her home to harm me. I described some of these experiences as having "life like a dark fabric with a fuchsia thread woven through it." I did not know the meaning of the fuchsia thread.

I did recall going to the hospital to be evaluated because I was so constipated on Black Friday (the day after Thanksgiving which until recently in mercantile terms meant the company was now in the black and everything until the end of the year was profit.) A medic consulted by phone suggested a dose of cod liver oil and a visit to the doctor on Monday. My mother followed directions. At the hospital, I do recall the doctor having my knees bent and my little feet (in the stirrups?) with a sheet draped over my thighs and legs. He examined me rectally. I went home.

Much of my later "child abuse" work was raging at the doctor. Why hadn't he recognized I had been sodomized? If he did recognize it, why didn't he do something about it? What had caused the molestation to stop?

My mother's best friend had accompanied us to the hospital where she was a volunteer. She went into the examining room with me (which I only learned when I was about 69 years of age!) My mother stayed in the waiting room. My mother's best friend was the wife of the man whose name I called out in the abreaction when I was 24: "Please_____ don't hurt me!"

I can imagine some would posit these traumas as the causes of my obesity.

It would be easier if that were the case. But at 52 years of age when I stopped eating grain and sugar in addition to the alcohol from which I had abstained since I was 24, my cravings left me. I had known a few short periods of freedom from "the phenomenon of craving"[5] when I had attempted to comply with various diets excluding grain and sugar. I always hoped I would be one of those normal people when I got to a normal weight. I would pick up the grain and sugar and found myself no longer normal in weight or any other way! My mental, emotional, physical, and spiritual reality changed radically when I put grain or sugar in my body.

I had succeeded in many aspects of my career, relationships, and life and had failed to achieve my goals in other areas important to me, until I stopped putting any grain or sugar into my body. The transformation was utterly remarkable. I had struggled with weight all my life and had 224 pounds on a 5 foot 4 ½ inch frame. I had dieted, climbed Mount Whitney, and walked a marathon in the year prior to changing my eating of grain and sugar. I was earnestly trying to lose weight. I was at 199 pounds after one year of these substantial efforts. Having ceased to put grain or sugar into my body as a result of suicidal intentions (no longer ideation), the direct result of a pint of cookie dough ice cream, I discarded 75 pounds in seven months. My body apparently cannot tolerate grain or sugar!

My belief and my experience: freedom comes with abstinence from triggering substances and behaviors. Still living in the body so much

---

[5]   Dr. Silkworth and the "Doctor's Opinion" Alcoholics Anonymous

smaller than my top weight and with clarity of mind and choices, I am transformed. I am grateful. I share these experiences to offer hope for new solutions.

Other actions may be necessary to support the continuation of abstinence over time; however, **abstinence from trigger foods and behaviors** are the basis needed to accomplish all the other tasks. I enjoy and delight in my life today. I am living!

FIRST THINGS FIRST

First things first, means to me I am a man who wears size 34 jeans (size 35 if I want to be intellectually honest) because more than ten years ago I reluctantly entered into a way of living that finally sunk a hook into me. Almost two and a half years ago, and after many moons of defiance, not reliance, I slowly stood on the precipice of food laden doom again and again. I now weigh and measure my food in all situations and circumstances. First things first, means to me I am a man who pulls out his kitchen scale at a recent Christening party, where I became a Godfather for the first time. Last summer I was able to show up at the hospital to see my nephew being born, about twenty minutes after I ate my weighed and measured dinner, and five minutes after I committed my three meals for the next day to my adviser in this way of life. First things first means that as a sweaty, lustful, self-obsessed man, who is a chronic compulsive eater and a human being who has gained and lost well over a hundred pounds, four or five times in one lifetime, I must maintain and grow my inner spiritual life so I can continue to weigh and measure my food happily and gratefully. When I don't, my body invariably returns to that hopeless, morbidly obese place of no peace and active food addiction.

When weighing and measuring is not first, then that queer idea occurs to me, like some slithering snake in the Garden of Eden, and my life falls apart. In 2007, after weighing and measuring for over two years, when thoughts attacked me like cloudbursts from above, a manifestation of my season of Saint Thomas, the doubts drove me. When the addict believes the lies from his or her head, the ideas usually enter in the ear, from an outside source. I compare my insides using the barometer of someone else's outsides, and awful things tend to happen. I stop weighing and measuring, and it works for a while, until it doesn't. My mind believes my decision was sound until I start changing the rules, again and again, to fit what I then believe. The rules are always in flux, as is my body. Size 32 jeans become size 38, and that becomes okay again, for some reason. Soon months and months go by, I am a size 42 again, and I think to myself, "That isn't so bad because I am still able to buy clothes at a regular store." At the end of this timeline of self-deception, I am back at my top weight, well over 300 pounds, but now closer to 350, and so the mailman comes, and I tear open the plastic packages, the ones from a catalog. What is inside is the size I was before, size 48 pants and 4XL shirts, and I can't believe it. This is what happens when my pride doesn't allow me to weigh and measure my food gratefully.

First things first, means I am a man who firmly believes weighing and measuring my food is the single most revolutionary act I perform on any given day. It is the primary reason I can be a man and all that that entails, in a normal sized body, without the apparent albatrosses of the morbidly obese. I don't weigh and measure my food as a solitary person because when I do that, I forget why I am doing it. I do it with a community which reminds me how important it is.

If you are as hopeless with your food addictions as I was, but you cannot possibly imagine framing an argument in your mind for doing what myself and so many others have discovered, I wish you well. I had tried everything else, to no avail. However, if you have reached that confused place, and you are wondering if such a radical yet simple solution, like weighing and measuring your food could be the cure for what ails you, then I encourage you to seek what we have found. When we do this first, and it becomes the most important thing in our lives, we have found our lives change 180 degrees. It is absolutely astonishing.

R.

I don't remember exactly when I started overeating, but I guess it was between ages 8 and 10. Through the years this progressed. During school years, I secretly bought myself food (ice cream, chips, chocolates, sweets and other things) and ate it hidden so my parents couldn't see. The urge to eat became stronger and stronger, and I didn't understand it. From the beginning, I didn't even know what was going on. I ate and read, and I couldn't stop eating. More and more thoughts were around food: how to get it, how to get money for food, how to steal it at home, where to hide it, and where to hide the wraps. From time to time my parents found things, and I was ashamed. I always promised I wouldn't do it again, but I couldn't stop, and I was gaining weight.

Through the coming years, I tried diets or healthier ways of eating, but I couldn't stay with either for long. The obsession with food and the urge to eat were so strong. I was thinking while at school or later when I finished with lectures, "I'll buy food and eat it." I always felt remorse, guilt, and shame afterward. In my twenties, I researched what was going on because I didn't understand it. I just needed to overeat and binge, and I couldn't stop.

By reading books, I discovered I was addicted to food; however, the knowledge about diets, about healthy ways of eating, about eating disorders, and about the fact I'm addicted to food didn't help me manage my problem and didn't help me to stop. Later I found a program and got a little bit of help, but the overeating continued, and any lost weight returned quickly.

I started therapy, and more and more discoveries were coming up about traumatic experiences in childhood, about a lack of trust and support, and about hidden, not yet recognized anxiety and depression from my childhood and teen years. Nobody realized I needed help then. It was all about losing weight. With food, I suppressed my feelings, pains, and everything. All this I did unconsciously.

Even with all the knowledge, I could not stop overeating until I had a defined plan of abstinence along with weighing my meals. The definition of my abstinence was set from an outside source - not from inside myself. I have only three meals with no grains, no sugars, and specific choices of foods. It is clearly written as to what is yes and what is no. I have defined amounts of protein, vegetables, fat, or fruit at meals, and I know at which meal what I eat. I need to abstain from overeating and from bingeing. I have been at a normal weight now for more than ten years, and I maintain the loss of approximately 64 pounds from my highest weight. I am not cured at all. The wishes for food and some mental obsession still exist, but with clearly defined abstinence, I manage to go through life without overeating or bingeing and without guilt or shame around food.

For me it would not be enough just to exclude sugars, grains, or starches for my food addiction is too advanced and too strong. I need the amounts to be defined, to know what is allowed and what is not, and I need to know how many times a day to eat. With abstinence, there is open space to deal, in therapy, with problems arising from suppressed feelings, the past, and the present of daily life. All this is essential for me: to get help and support for what I'm doing and who I am.

BINGEING

I am fifty years old and all my life I have struggled with an obsession with food: food in my thoughts, food in my refrigerator, and the food all around me. When there was a special season, for instance, Christmas, I stood in the stores and looked at those fantastic things wrapped in fancy gold paper, and I couldn't take my eyes off the food.

When and how did it start? I remember one evening, when I was nine, how my mother after a tough day, stood on a scale and with a disappointed whisper, she would say, "I should lose weight."

I stood on the scale too, and in my mind was the same thought: "I want to lose weight." Since then, I think I have obsessed with rituals around eating: how to eat, what to eat, and when to eat.

In my high school, I developed a habit of bingeing. I did not eat in the morning and then would overeat in the afternoon. I started trying many diets, losing weight and gaining weight. I always gained more weight than I lost. At the end of my study in another city, I had gained 100 kilos.

But I was young then, and my metabolism still responded when putting my body on any diet I read had worked for other people. I had started to exercise abnormally, eat healthy food, and lose a lot of weight. But when this period was over, because all those periods would somehow pass, I would start to overeat. I then developed bulimia. I was not a young girl anymore. I thought I had found a solution to my problems, which was obesity; being fat. I thought this was the problem all my life.

When I was thirty, I was exhausted with these rituals. I was literally on the edge of my "living capacity." After bingeing and vomiting, I was sometimes so tired I couldn't stand on my feet. When I read of the solution to such a problem in a newspaper, I first started to search for help from other people. I managed to stop vomiting but not overeating.

Over the next ten years, I gained a lot of weight and ended with 122 kilos (371.8 pounds), unable to move, to work, and to think other thoughts than how to lose this weight. My body was older and didn't respond to diets anymore. Anyway, I couldn't stick to any diet for more than two hours.

I had to start to search for help again. I am very stubborn, and that's why it took me so many years to find it. I always thought I just had to lose weight and everything in my life would be just fine, almost like paradise on earth. I never thought I had an eating disorder or that my eating habits and rituals were a problem. I always looked for the cause of my food addiction outside of me.

When I came to another self-help program, I had a hard time admitting to myself that I was a food addict. Still, sometimes I pity myself, but I am here and have gained another opportunity in life to be useful to others and to work and to stay at a normal body size.

When I think of my way out of obesity and out of being in the food 24 hours a day and 7 days a week, I can genuinely say, "Seek, and you shall find. Ask, and it shall be given" (Bible.)

Now, after ten years in the program, I can say to myself, "This is food addiction, not real hunger, and it is hard to overcome these thoughts, but not impossible." I also know I can't and I will never be able to fight this illness on my own.

M

FOOD: THE SHADOW SIDE OF ALCOHOLISM

Managing my functional alcoholism before my sobriety involved different strategies. One of them was constructing a pact with another devil – food. I discovered if I drank a "moderate" amount of alcohol and then turned to my favorite foods (like cake and twizzlers) for a "moderate" amount, I could get through an evening without overdoing either. Sometimes I could settle for food and leave alcohol behind completely. But it seemed I suffered the fewest consequences whenever I found the 'happy balance' of both.

This 'program' of controlled co-use had worked for me ever since I returned to school and found the need to curb my drinking. It was the perfect compromise between my need to soothe myself with something and my need to reduce the consequences of getting either too drunk or too caught up in a bulimic cycle.

One particular evening I hosted a party. I had already drunk my designated share of alcohol for the night, and I was still feeling loud and boisterous. The party was not over yet.

Putting down my martini glass, I headed for the buffet. I piled my plate with cookies and nuts and chunks of high-priced cheese, knowing I would soon slip downstairs to the basement laundry room where I could purge. I would probably do so a few times over the course of the evening. This was my pattern: four double-double drinks and four binge-purge cycles usually got me through a party night.

Later, downstairs, I was in a panic. Sometimes I just couldn't vomit quickly. I worried I would be away from the party for too long. How would I explain my disappearance? I heaved and heaved, jabbed my fingers to the back of my throat, only grateful that the basement door was locked and the noise of the dancing and shouting upstairs hid the sound of my efforts to retch. I started to whimper aloud with frustration.

"What's wrong?"

Mortified, I turned and saw an old friend staring at me with a mixture of confusion, disbelief, and concern. "How did you get in here?" I coughed. At first, I was more embarrassed than I had ever felt before; then I lashed out: "This isn't what you think!"

He sputtered that my partner had given him the keys to the basement door so he could get for the drinks more ice from our deep freeze.

"This isn't what you think," I repeated. My eyes dropped. I could not look directly at him. The shame was too overpowering. Sometimes the shame of my behavior around food felt worse than the shame of my drinking.

Using food to control my drinking ultimately failed. When I got so embarrassed by my feral relationship to food, I found myself back daydreaming about alcohol again. The glamour of drinking beckoned and before I knew it, I was planning to skulk back to the bar down the street, hopefully unnoticed by anyone I knew. It was not until I made the commitment to stop both alcohol and compulsive consumption of food I finally was relieved of the obsession to drink or overeat. Thirty years it took to recognize food as the shadow side of my alcoholism.

SURRENDERED AND NEARLY A
300-POUND WEIGHT CHANGE

I know I have surrendered to Step One in this 12 Step program because I feel peace around my food today. This is peace I previously did not have. I can sometimes think I've lost that peace, for example, when lunch or dinner seems a long time away, and I want it now. However, I don't lose the surrender if I don't act on the thoughts and instead continue to weigh and measure my food without exception. I also reach out and hand over my concerns to fellow program members. I love the saying: "There is always another meal coming!"

With a surrender to Step One, ("We admitted we were powerless over food—that our lives had become unmanageable.) a new clarity comes to me. I am powerless over food, people, places, and situations. I learn through surrender that it is only by letting go and letting God that I can live more fully in the present. Today I have a program of recovery from compulsive eating that works. I have a loving sponsor, a loving community, and a new loving relationship with myself. I have increased clarity, particularly with my behavior around food. If I remember and continue to weigh and measure without exception, I trust I can remain abstinent, one day at a time, for the rest of my life. Living in the present moment here and now, I find freedom.

When I first came into this program years ago, I weighed 460 pounds and was almost unable to move. I failed to live a normal functioning life. Incapable of taking care of my personal needs, I faced the real possibility of living the rest of my life in full-time nursing care, unable to walk or breathe comfortably. I was trapped, not only trapped in a physical body that imprisoned me, but more importantly in a relationship with food that sucked me further down into my self-destruction. I felt utterly hopeless; there was no way out; and there was no one or anything that could save me. I was waiting to die. Today more than nine years later, my life has completely turned around quite simply because I continue to follow the program without exception, no matter what is going on in my life. I do this one day at a time.

Since coming into this 12-step program, I have had many "first time in my life" experiences. I graduated from college, survived breast cancer, traveled twice across the Atlantic Ocean to the US, and traveled to several European and African countries. I have climbed mountains in more ways than one and successfully lost over 300 pounds in weight and have maintained that loss for more than five years.

Today I live in a body that allows me the freedom to live an independent and free life. I am free to travel independently. Today my mind is free of food obsession. Today food is in its place. I get to eat three delicious, abundant meals a day with nothing in between. It is an amazing life compared to the life I used to live when I first arrived in this 12-step program. I felt hopeless and alone then, but today, I am no longer alone. I have found a Higher Power that is always with me, and I am part of a 12-step community. I am full of gratitude and H O P E = Happy Our Program Exists.

POWERLESSNESS

I remember, sometimes multiple times daily, I am powerless over compulsive eating and the lure of sweets and carbohydrates. The consequences of indulging are devastating to my self-worth and desire to live. When I relapsed, I crossed the line. I tried and could not get back for eight years. I could not trust myself to get through breakfast abstinently. My work meant nothing, and once I started eating, I could not stop and didn't want to. I need to remember I was enslaved to food every waking hour. I choose to remember the illusion of enjoying sweets and carbohydrates is just that – an illusion. Telling myself, I will eat delicious food is a lie. When I relapsed, I ate tasteless bags of food, and nothing was good. I went for the junk because I couldn't wait to prepare delicious food.

Today I go grocery shopping, which is still not my favorite task. I know if I do not shop and keep myself supplied with abstinent food, I am in danger of discarding it all to go back to compulsively eating. Admitting I am powerless over food is a daily reminder of the dire consequences I face if I choose no longer to be abstinent.

AM I A FOOD ADDICT?

Yes, I am a food addict. I do not believe there was any time in my life when I demonstrated normal eating. My mother described me as, "liking sugar, but all children like sugar coatings." At 18 months of age, I was with my grandparents, and I have a picture of my face covered with chocolate from a pan my grandmother had used to make fudge. That is one of my earliest photographs and probably my first indication I was a food addict. I had problems with weight management from the beginning of my life. I was not overweight as a young child because my mother was a home economics major and consistently managed our family's eating. She fed us well and did everything she was able to do to control our weight and health.

My weight gain and cycles of weight gain started when I was old enough to escape my mother's watchful eye. First, I stole food and adult beverages from the coffee table (grinders and beer) when I was 5. (I remember I knew it was wrong.) Then, I ate at school. I was a little chubby as a seven-year-old in pictures, and it went on from there. I ate whenever I could. When I was with my father, we ate pistachio ice cream with chocolate chips, popcorn, sandwiches, sweet cinnamon rolls, and large amounts of sugar and quantities of whatever was available. Mother did not know. It was "our secret."

I made unhealthy choices regularly because I would always opt for sugar with a grain, if possible. My favorite foods from a very young age included potatoes with homemade egg noodles. The noodles came from my Welsh-Palatinate heritage and were made from egg and flour along with gravy that came from cooked roast beef juices. The mashed potatoes were put on the plate with the noodles placed on top, with gravy on top of that and a little piece of meat. For dessert then my favorite was white cake with lemon frosting and filling or carrot cake with thick cream cheese frosting.

Great amounts of fudge were always a favorite. Pancakes and syrup with a little bit of egg were later some of my happiest memories. My grandmother made Krispy crème-like donuts from scratch. She made buttermilk twists (flour, sugar, cream.) I loved her and her baking.

As I entered junior high school, my favorites included French Fries and the opportunity to eat secretly the things other people could get. I would hide food in my bedroom. As I got older, I hid food in the car, and my eating increased in frequency and quantity until my late teens. I struggled trying to restrict **and** trying to increase my food quantities. I did both. I restricted from morning until late at night at the beginning of college. I ate huge amounts of food unless I was at the sorority house, in which case I would eat cautiously and moderately under other people's eyes.

My weight increased as a college freshman from an almost normal weight (under my mother's supervision) to an obese weight. I gained between 30 and 40 pounds in my first year of college. I was dismayed by this and was powerless over food and my cravings. I ate dozens of donuts from the local donut store. I wanted to exercise but I had a lot of physical difficulties which prohibited my attempts to exercising with skill or care. (I was uncoordinated. I needed adaptive PE before such classes existed.)

I didn't purge except for one time. It was a time a sculptor visited me and I had overeaten and was physically uncomfortable. I thought, "If I could just get rid of this...." So, I tried to vomit but nothing came out. I looked in the mirror after having tried repeatedly and saw I had two black eyes. I must have broken the blood vessels around my eyes, and consequently, I looked at that and thought, "Okay, God doesn't want me to do this." (This was the ONLY time I ever stopped doing a self-harming action after one attempt.)

My late stage addiction included severe consequences. I was morbidly obese; my feet hurt; I had chronic depression; and I wanted to die. Then the day came when I did, in fact, decide I was at a critical stage. I was dealing with the effects of one pint of Ben & Jerry's Chocolate Chip Cookie Dough ice cream, and the next morning when I woke up my brain was foggy, my joints were aching, my feet felt as though I had broken them, and every part of my body ached. I had a plan, the means, and the determination to kill myself that day. I had not gotten out of bed yet.

I "heard" a voice say, "Go to a meeting." At that point, I got up and went to a 12-step meeting because I was aware my life was in jeopardy. I'd spent 27 years of my adult life trying to find a solution to my food addiction and could not find one. I had tried everything: all the traditional things like a food loss program, multiple self-help groups, and all sorts of other things. The only things that had worked, to any degree, had been the stimulants from the diet doctor in the 60's and one plan on a grey paper in 1971. I had some success with a diet, but the ketosis and the smells were too much. I had success with amphetamines and diet pills. I looked like a victim when the rainbow diet pill scare hit the news. The diet doctor was willing to continue prescribing, but I knew I could not continue.

What happened? I went to one flavor of self-help group and I got an address for a another self-help support group meeting. That day I started that recovery program, and I'm nearly 100 pounds less in weight than I was then. I had tried everything but found what works for me, and I surrendered to the fact my scale and my weighed and measured food make a difference in my life beyond anything I had ever tried consistently before. I am powerless over food (grains, sugar, and alcohol), and my life had become unmanageable. The only thing that allows me peace is my surrender to a power greater than myself. I choose to call that Spirit, Universe, Higher Power, and Mother/Father God I am committed to consistency. Also, the peace comes from my scale which allows me to weigh and measure my food along with a cup and tablespoon. I turn over my food to a person I trust, in the way she requests it of me, which is in agreement with her trusted person. We are a team which then I can offer as I support the network of others.

I continue to do this one meal at a time, and I am eternally grateful to say I no longer fight the food wars. I am a person who has lost jobs and who had been unable to work and/or maintain healthy relationships because of my insatiable cravings for specific foods and other behaviours.

There isn't anything, in the final stage of food addiction I have not done and experienced, except for death. I stole food when I was young and did so throughout my life. I lied and cheated to create circumstances in which I could eat with impunity. I pressed people out of my life if they got in the way of my desired consumption. Food came first. It came between me and the world. At first it seemed to protect me, and then it turned on me and destroyed the essence of me. These are the awkward details that form the reality: I'm a food addict and will always be a food addict. Some say once a cucumber has become a pickle, there is no way to return to being a cucumber. I may have been a pickle at birth or at least as early as that 18-month old with fudge all over my face. If it takes consumption of sugar and/or grain to initiate the addiction, then I may have started as a toddler; otherwise, it may have been keen at birth. I have a genetic history on both sides: mother's parents and my father and his parents and back through my genealogy.

27 years of trying to find a different way than abstaining completely from grain, sugar and alcohol, made it possible for me to know what doesn't work. Abstinence from those substances coupled with weighing and measuring my food to be certain I eat <u>enough</u> food now address the physical. Addressing the emotional, I use recovery tools in my help group. These offer a roadmap and as I repeated work over the decades, I have grown up.

Specifically, participating in communities of service-oriented individuals dedicating their lives to aiding and enhancing the lives of their fellows creates fellowship and a sense of belonging I sought throughout my life. My brain works when I do not cloud it with foods to which I have "allergic" reactions (getting hyped up or falling asleep or getting ravenously hungry two hours after eating them.) I no longer need to be perfect to survive. I am a perfect Child of God **and** an imperfect human being. I am enough. I make mistakes; however, I'm not a mistake. I carry neither shame nor guilt. I have a disease and it is in remission due to choices I make.

I have specific foods and beverages I do not put into my body. As a result, I am FREE from the mental, emotional, physical, and spiritual challenges which plagued me for more than fifty years. I encourage people to address food issues earlier than I did, and then to stay abstinent from those substances to which their individual bodies respond negatively. Continuing to grow and mature and care for oneself supports a life beyond those I dreamed in the days before I became hopeless. I have successfully let go of multiple behaviors dues to my beffoged brain cleared.

I love today. I live today. I enjoy the bliss of skiing and dancing, the contentment of a relationship my spouse and I have worked to achieve and maintain, and a productive life I value as I pass on what I have learned to others who wish to learn and grow and change. Yes, I am a food addict in recovery one day at the time.

Hi, my name is M, a grateful, abstinent compulsive overeater. I'm delighted to be here this morning. I love conventions and being amongst people who understand me. I first want to say this is my story. I don't speak for _A and please take what you like and leave the rest. The topic today is from Relapse to Recovery.

If _A had a poster child for relapse, it would be my picture on the poster. The best thing I did for myself was to keep coming back, even in relapse. I had tried leaving once before, and that didn't work out at all.

I first came to _A in July 1983. I heard something wonderful at that first meeting: I had a disease, and it wasn't my fault. I couldn't stop overeating. It felt like a significant weight came off my shoulders. Some of the guilt and shame around the food was relieved. But I still had a long way to go.

I was the middle child of a family that showed love through food. I don't remember hearing, "I love you". I do remember hearing, "Eat this, it will make you feel better. Eat this and stop crying." However, I know my family loved me. But I needed more because that's what I have - a disease of more. I never had enough. More is always better. I'm still working on that today.

I stayed in _A for around seven years. For about five minutes my weight got down to 125 pounds. I was great at telling my story and being on the speaker circuit, but I never worked the steps. So, of course, I started overeating again, and the weight came back on, plus bonus pounds. Eventually, I left.

I guess I needed to do more research. Misery, hopelessness, helplessness, despair, pity, and shame were abundant in my life.

I was a single mother raising two sons on my own. The food was my friend, and it helped me through many a difficult situation. *"We will not regret the past nor wish to shut the door on it."* That promise has come true for me. I don't know if I could have gone on without the mind-blowing numbness that overeating provided me. Food was my friend, until it was not.

It eventually became a more significant problem than what I thought. Then by the Grace of God, I accidentally received a phone call from someone in _A. She was looking for another M. and got me on the phone. That was all the push I needed to come back. Thank you, God.

It was now 1997, and my weight was at an all-time high of 242 pounds. I was done researching and hit the ground running. I knew I had to work the steps to be successful. But what does that mean? Work the steps? I heard that repeatedly, but still, it was unclear to me what to do.

So, the first thing I did was get a sponsor and call her. That's important. You can have a sponsor, but if you don't call her, it won't work.

I started at the beginning with Step One: *"We admitted we were powerless over food -- that our lives had become unmanageable"*. Well, I thought I had that down pat. Easy. Look at me. Overweight, and couldn't stop eating once I started. One chocolate bar! Are you kidding? I always wanted more. And more and more. The principle behind Step One is honesty, and that's hard for me. To tell someone what I put in my mouth and ate provoked just too much shame and guilt. Then -- my life unmanageable? How could that be? I worked hard to support myself and my children, even having two jobs for over ten years. But was I excelling or just getting by? I would yell at my kids when all they wanted was my attention. I buried my anger and fear in fake cheerfulness. Everyone said I had a nice smile. If they could see inside me, they would be surprised. I need to remind myself every day I am powerless over food.

Step Two says *"Came to believe that a power greater than ourselves could restore us to sanity."* I was so out of control with the food, but I kept on turning to it to feel better. The principle behind Step Two is hope, and an acronym for Hope is "Hearing Other People's Experiences." Finally, I believe there is an answer to my allergy of the body and obsession of the mind.

Step Three is *"Made a decision to turn our will and our lives over to the care of God as we understood Him."* I love Step Three because it states, "care of God as we understood Him." Not a Jewish God, not a Christian God, no religious God: A God of my understanding who loves me unconditionally. He has my picture on his refrigerator. And I turn my will and my life over to His care. Care. God cares about me. He wants what's best for me.

The principle behind Step Three is faith. An acronym for Faith is a "Fantastic Adventure in Trusting Him." One of the promises of Step Three is, "Once we ... truly take the third step, we cannot fail to recover." Wow, "we cannot fail to recover." What a great promise! I know it's true because it is happening to me.

Like I said, I came back to _A, nearly twenty years ago. Wow. I got a sponsor and started working with her. I made a minimum of five telephone calls a day. At the time, I was working full-time, spending approximately three hours a day back-and-forth to work, and raising two boys. My offspring were 20 and 16 years old at that time. So not little children, thank you, God. Who did I call? Anybody. I didn't care. I got names from the list and called. I often hear the excuse, "I can't call somebody I don't know. What if they're busy?" I didn't care. Or I hear "What will we talk about?" A good topic of discussion is always what step you are on today?

I just did it. This built-up an incredible network of _A friends, people who understood me and who did similar things with food as I did. I could turn to them when a crisis hit. When my job became redundant. My boss was as upset as I was, while telling me the bad news. What did I do when I left work that day? I drove straight to my sponsor's house to talk to her. She had a simple solution: I could either live in fear or live in faith: my choice. And thank you, God I chose faith. Sure enough, I got another job at the hospital, and this one was a big promotion.

I celebrated five years of abstinence. And then it went downhill. I started dating and spent less time doing my program work. Recovery and God were not my priorities.

Good years and bad years followed. My older sister passed away. So here I was 55, retired, and newly re-married. It was a scary time for me and fear of economic insecurity was always on my shoulder.

In the next ten years, I worked the program somewhat haphazardly. Slipping and sliding: weight back up, then down again. One and a half years of abstinence and another big weight loss before I gave away my abstinence again. But this time I never left _A. I kept coming back. I always had hope that somehow, someday I would get it. Abstinence brings peace and contentment and they weren't there.

After that, I never really had more than three months in a row abstaining. Two years ago, I went on a great holiday with my sister to England and on a 12-day cruise to many countries. It was fantastic. When we arrived back in England my sister went home, and I continued my travels on my own for two weeks. The good life, eh? The food was OK, for the most part. When I returned home, I went into a depressing funk, and I couldn't figure out why.

Then, I heard about a pilot project for food addicts who were being admitted to a treatment center for three weeks. I was very excited about the news. I figured the only way for me to get abstinent was to lock me up! I got accepted into the program. Of course, the three weeks leading up to my admission I gained 10 pounds, because I figured I might as well eat everything now. Soon I wouldn't be able to do so. For once in my life, I ate lots of crap in front of others. I usually didn't do that: I was a sneaky, secretive eater, but now I just didn't care.

In December, I went to the treatment center. Remember at the beginning when I said this is my story? I don't speak for _A. We can get outside help. But I want to be clear. My recovery comes from _A, which brings God into my daily life. In treatment, we had a strict food plan: no sugar, no flour, no grains. Everything is weighed or measured. We met daily to work Steps 1 to 3. We attended meetings outside the house nearly every day. I had a food buddy to help me with the measuring, and we shared our feelings around the food. I tell you, it was too much food for me! It took me a long time to eat my meals. The good news was I was never hungry. (Although for me hunger, has nothing to do with my overeating.) I am obsessed with food, and my disease tells me "It's OK to eat just this little bit"; or "I'll start tomorrow"; or "I don't care"; and other lies.

Another benefit for me was the recipes I received for food I could eat on the go. I mean how could I drive to long distances without eating peanut butter sandwiches? So now I can prepare. You know that expression, "Failing to plan, is planning to fail?" I spent 21 days away from home, learning a new way of life. I lost 10 pounds in treatment and continued to lose. My total weight loss today is 75 pounds. What a miracle!

Another thing I've had to work on is my obsession with getting weighed. I couldn't wait to get below 200 pounds, then into the 80's, 70's, etc. I must learn I am responsible for the action and God is responsible for the results. My weight is none of my business. The size of my clothes is something else I'm working on. If a size 6 fit me in the past, I would just buy it. Who cares if I liked it? Thank you, God, I'm past that now.

So, what do I do to keep this recovery in my life? I work the steps. God is in my daily life. I use all the tools. I already talked about using the tool of having a plan of eating. I must tailor my food plan for me because I have an inflammatory bowel disease. The food plan I got in treatment calls for 36 ounces of vegetables a day. That's way too much for me. I have been in touch with the nutritionist who formulated this food plan, and he has been terrific and very helpful.

All my other years in the program, for the most part, my food plan was very "loosey-goosey" or very casual. I often said I followed a particular food guide when really, I was mostly eating what I thought

I could get away with. A strict food plan gives me freedom because I know what I can and cannot eat and the quantities. I don't want to give the impression I'm perfect because I'm not. I've had slips and volume problems. The one thing I do though is talk about it, be honest, and learn from the experience. I am a work in progress.

Another tool I love is literature. I especially love two daily readers. There is a lot of wisdom, lot of experience, strength, and hope. If you are having food thoughts, I challenge you to pick up any of the program literature and read for 10 minutes. Then check if you are still having food thoughts. If so, you then keep on reading. I know for me reading helps remind me of what I am doing and the many benefits of abstinence.

Earlier I talked about the telephone. I get so much out of making connections with my fellow compulsive overeaters. It's beneficial to build up a network of people we can turn to when times get bad or when we have wonderful news to share. Taking the phone list at meetings is an excellent way to start calling people if you are shy: it is a list of people who want you to call them.

I love meetings. I feel at home the minute I walk in the door. I've never been sorry for attending. Before _A all I wanted to do after dinner was sit in front of the TV and shovel in the food. That's not the way I live today.

Another tool I love is service. It helps me so much because when I came to _A, I was an egomaniac with an inferiority complex. I thought I was stupid, useless, and had no common sense. But doing service shows me I can do a good job. There is always someone out there to help or to help you if you ask. Have you heard that expression, "God doesn't choose the equipped; he equips the chosen"? It's true for me. Over the years I have done the following service positions: Intergroup rep, intergroup treasurer, regional rep, world service delegate, group treasurer, sponsor and all the things that anyone can do regardless of their abstinent date. I set up the meeting, put away chairs, have been the key person, and have taken care of the telephone list. There are lots of jobs to do, and we get a lot of benefit from service.

The tool of writing. Not my favorite one. I'm a talker, not a writer. But I do get a lot out of writing. I start every day with prayers, meditation, and writing. The first thing I write is five statements of gratitude. I believe gratitude is a small prayer. It's acknowledging the blessings I have received while asking God to continue helping me. One gratitude I often write is "Thank you God for my safe, return journey" or "Thank you God for the good health of my loved ones."

The tool of sponsorship is such a blessing, and it ties in with the slogan: "You are never alone." Often your sponsor is one of your first relationships in _A. You can never pick the wrong sponsor because if it doesn't work out, it's a learning experience. Once we're in the program, it's all a learning experience. I remember giving my sponsor my first fifth step. I was nervous and afraid she would judge me. We sat outside and asked God to be with us. It worked out fine. She didn't faint or act negatively. She shared some of her stories, and that was it. I could move on to step six. Being a sponsor is such a gift. Sponsees think I am helping them, but the truth is I get so much out of sponsoring.

The tool of anonymity protects us from our egos and makes us feel safe enough to share our deepest, innermost feelings. The newest tool is an action plan. It means what it says. We need to have an action plan in our lives. Plan what we eat, what step we are working on, what meetings we attend, etc. I like to have a plan, especially if a thought arises for me to eat something when I'm not hungry, or it's not a meal time. I need to get motivated to get the daily treatment for this fatal disease.

So, I have been following this food plan now for nearly two years. I go to three or four meetings a week. I work with a sponsor, and I am a sponsor. My life has turned completely upside down. I am feeling my feelings. Sometimes that's good, and sometimes it's not. But that's life. I have a good relationship with my sons and their partners. I'm crazy about my grandson and granddaughter. My daughter-in-law told me once that my granddaughter said, "Gram is my best friend." I am her Gram. How wonderful is that? I know if I hadn't changed my controlling ways, I would barely see that family, so I'm very grateful to God for showing me the way.

My life today is quite the adventure. Because I put my program and my abstinence first, I continue to live a full life. I am present in my life, and it just keeps getting better and better. Last fall I had the most marvelous travel experience ever possible. I was away from home for six months and mostly on my own. I flew to exotic places. God was always with me. I went to many meetings while I was away, including a convention and meetings on the cruise ship. Thank God for email and FaceTime so I could be in touch with my family and friends here. I drove nearly 10,000 km on the "wrong" side of the road! I was really being looked after. Thank you, God.

I continue to have many challenges in my life today— health problems, marital problems, and just life. God has proven to me over the years that He has my back, so I don't need to worry. Just buckle up for the ride.

The first food-related event I recall was when I was three or four years of age. I was at a sleepover at my aunt's house, and I got up in the middle of the night, went to the refrigerator, and ate the remainder of the dinner roast. The next morning my aunt looked in the fridge and saw the roast was gone. When she asked who had eaten the food I told her I had. My aunt had a shocked look on her face and, if I recall correctly, her mouth was open. Perhaps she could not believe this young child could have consumed the entire leftover roast, or maybe she was trying to figure out what she would substitute as lunch for her husband. It was the first time I realized I was not like everyone else. I was different from the rest.

I was different, and that's why I wet the bed. I was different, and that is why I had to bribe other kids to play with me. I was different, and that's why the pedophile chose me. I didn't look like the others. I didn't sound like the others. I was off-kilter. I believe this feeling of "differentness" contributed to my propensity to do things I thought would make me fit in: things like sneaking cigarettes and shoplifting. I was cured early of my short-lived shoplifting career when the store security escorted me to a private room and called local law enforcement. The judge told me he never wanted to see my face again, and he didn't! I wish I could say the same about the cigarettes, but it took over thirty years for me to let them go.

Every year I got heavier and heavier. I remember saying I would never weigh two-hundred pounds, but I did. After I crossed the two-hundred-pound mark, I said that I would never weigh two-hundred and fifty pounds, but I did. I believe I don't have a top weight. It has been truthfully said by others, "My top weight is dead." I have no doubt I could eat myself into an early grave. Diabetes, high blood pressure, and the myriad of other diseases directly related to obesity could easily be my fate, a slow, pain-filled death. I remember fearing I would one day get so large I would no longer be able to fit through the door and a hole would have to be cut in the side of the house to drag me out.

I believed if I could just lose the excess weight, all my life problems would be solved. I would put off participating in activities or seeing certain people, in hopes I would lose some weight first. During one of my "thin" phases, I met THAT guy! We were driving in opposite directions, and we saw each other, and it was an instant attraction. We were young and in lust, and our romance was good while it lasted. Even after we broke up, we remained friends, talked on the telephone, and had a close platonic relationship.

My friend asked me out, but I wouldn't go because once again I was in a heavy phase. I figured I would lose some weight and then I would go out with him. I was just too heavy to be seen. I regret that decision because my friend died of an aneurysm. We will never have that chance to meet and talk.

I was an avid watcher of infomercials, looking for the "cure" or the new and improved fix. What have I tried? I tried eating protein supplements, fasting, eating only one of type food, liquid diets, "pay as you go" food programs, mental self-flagellation, prayer, and hypnotism to name a few. The question with the shortest answer is "What haven't I tried?"

There came a time when nothing worked. I was in a support group where I lost weight and then gained back every pound, plus ten more for good measure. I "slipped" (losing weight and regaining and gaining more and losing abstinence again and again) in those rooms for seven years, but the good news is I did not leave. I kept coming back. A lady I sponsored was now sponsoring me, and she suggested we go to another food group to get a copy of their food program, and perhaps I could get abstinent again. We went to the meeting, and for some reason, I stayed.

I was beaten, desperate, and I was ready to sign up for whatever I was told to do. I was told I must weigh and measure all my food, all the time -- at home, in a restaurant, no matter where, and no matter what. And it worked!

I began to detox, and the negative voices in my head started to silence. It's funny; I remember a person sharing she weighed and measured without exception and she did not eat grains. I felt sorry for that poor confused woman, and now I am blessed to be similarly "confused"!

I have been living this way of life for many meals. Does this mean my life is perfect and all my problems have magically disappeared? No, not so. My cousin who was reared with me died. I had abdominal surgery. I had knee surgery. My only child died. My mother had to be placed in a care facility because of her dementia. The latest "life adventure" included a total knee replacement and a stay in a convalescent hospital. All these events occurred but did not give me an excuse to NOT weigh and measure my food. I never want to give up the clarity of mind that weighing and measuring have afforded me. I weigh and measure no matter what – without exception.

MY JOURNEY TO RECOVERY

I was told that at six months old my mother would give me a bottle when I could not fall asleep and when I continued screaming she gave me another one. I guess, from a very young age, I had issues with food. Probably some of it was genetic; however, I was probably putting out a signal my mom was reading incorrectly and treated it by stuffing a bottle in my mouth. So, I learned, at a very young age, having something in my mouth was comfort. I have absolutely no recollection of any of this, but these are stories shared to me by mom. What I do know is one day when I was doing a body-mind technique with a therapist, I began to remember being very, very angry in my body. That's how I realized what happened when I was younger and was able to connect the dots.

When I was four, I have a memory of being in a ballet class with other girls my age. There were two rows of us lined up. I remember looking at each one of the girls and thinking, "I am fat." Through all the work I have done over the years as well as having a clear thought process—not having a foggy brain due to the influence of my drug (sugar & food), I have come to realize that my four-year old brain equated fat as bad and weak and thin as good and strong.

My older brother was a goodie two shoes kind of a kid who played the piano, did all the right things, and was skinny thin. I, on the other hand, was mischievous, climbed trees, and got mud on my pretty pink and white dress my mother had made for me. I remember hearing all the time, "He this, he that, and she doesn't!" The differences between us were the equation that stuck in my head. Also, my mom was always thin, and in my head, I thought something must be wrong with me because I was not thin. Becoming thin became an issue for me from a very young age because I thought thin was good and thin was strong.

Today, looking back at pictures of that four-year-old little girl, I know she was not fat. It was completely up in my head and in my misperception of my body and body image. I feel badly because my misperceptions contributed to a major lack of self-confidence for a kid who was already very shy and insecure.

When I was eight, my family moved and relocated to another country. This is when I believe my active compulsive eating started. I know it was there already because I believe I was born with the predisposition to becoming an addict. I know today addiction "is a primary, chronic disease of the brain, reward, motivation, memory and related circuitry. Dysfunction in these circuits leads to characteristic biological, psychological, social and spiritual manifestations." This is exactly what the Big Book of Alcoholics Anonymous states and I believe it to be true.

When my compulsive eating began, I remember sneaking and taking food from the refrigerator and saying, "Oh, but the cat must have eaten it," or "Oh, but the dog must have eaten it." I even sorted the items to make it look as though no one had touched them but my mom obviously knew someone was eating the food. I think my mother knew I was stealing the food, but she never confronted me. So, from the very young age of eight or nine, guilt and shame became my familiar "acquaintances."

At the ripe old age of 14, because I was one of the heaviest kids in the class, I decided it was time to do something about my weight. I was often made fun of which did not help my insecurity, lack of self-esteem, and of course my "buddies" guilt and shame! So, I decided to try a weight loss program. I went with a friend and for the first couple of weeks it was like a honeymoon. In the beginning, I lost some weight but then I would gain it back. I also had bad PMS so every four weeks when I ovulated, no matter what diet I was on or not on, I ended up bingeing and gaining weight. Today, I understand my hormones were completely out of whack contributing to my lack of "success" losing weight and keeping it off. However, in that "era" it was a subject that was not discussed so I had no idea what was happening.

I must have been about 16 when I discovered compulsive exercising as a means to control my weight. It did not do much for my weight, but I liked the effect. Also, I think exercising compulsively gave me a false sense of being in control. At some point, unable to control the large quantities of food I binged on (an example of the progression of the disease and tolerance), desperate to lose weight and be thin, I tried laxatives. However, I did not like the lack of control I had in the timing of taking the pills and needing to use the rest room. Was I a control freak or what! So, after a relatively short time I stopped using them.

When I was 18 or 19, I visited a cousin of mine at her University dorm. I vividly remember her roommate speaking with her about eating and throwing up. For me, the seed was planted, and it sprouted shortly after. I tried it. Although it was not great fun, throwing up was an amazing way to get rid of the food. Being the perfectionist, I am, over the years, as it did not happen immediately, I perfected my technique and got it down to a science! (As I know today, it was the progression of the disease.) I knew what to eat, what not to eat, and was able to combine foods that would make me throw up more easily or not throw up. I learned the "correct" timing. If I ate A, then I should drink something bubbly, so I would be able to throw up easily and if I ate B, then I had so much time until I needed to do my thing, etc.

Today, when I think back, it makes me feel very sad because I was only a teenager. At that time, I believed the main thing was to get rid of all the food, so I would lose weight or at least not gain. At one point I even got thinner than my mother! To me, it was like, "Yes!" It was a real goal in my life. It did not matter that my throat was ripped and bleeding and that it was costing me my teeth and my general health. Nothing mattered because I was going to be thin come hell or high water.

At University, with the tension of exams, having the need to do well, and the perfectionist in me, I discovered I could starve myself and create an excellent high. During exams, I lived on coffee, sugar, and sugary gum. So, I was a little bit crazy, just a little!! During this period of time, food and weight became all-consuming. It was this diet or that diet; it was the bananas and milk diet, it was the grape diet, or it was the grapefruit diet. I would not eat at all and starve myself or I would binge and gain weight and start throwing up again. What I was doing to myself was absolutely crazy! I reached a point where even if I wanted to, I could not stop. It was beyond my control!

I was in denial and knew it; however, I was unwilling to admit it to myself or anyone else. I kept up my bulimic behavior for 15 years without telling a soul. No one knew. Like I said, I was a perfectionist, so I perfected the ways I could sneak food as well as how to rid myself of it. I would take my roommate's food and then while everyone was asleep vomit and get rid of the waste in garbage bags! You name it, I did it. So, on the one hand, there was this high like, "Yes, I did it. I got rid of all the food and I am staying thin!" On the other hand, I was in incredible pain as to where I was in my life. Socially I was isolating, academically I was flourishing, but my life revolved around my binging and my purging. Binge, purge, work, study—that was my life! I remember how painful it was.

I was hospitalized twice as a result of my binging and purging. The first time I experienced generalized aches and pains throughout my body. The second time I experienced tingling and numbness in my face and hands, which scared me. It turned out to be a life-threatening situation. My electrolytes were seriously out of whack and if untreated my heart could have stopped beating. Deep down, I knew what was causing my problems, but I could not stop what I was doing with the food. My rationale was I worked in a hospital and if I went into cardiac arrest, they could just rush me to the Emergency Room.

I first heard of _A when I was around 18 years old, from a friend of my parents. I thought, "That's for those sick people, I can just learn how to eat properly on my own." Well, ten years later, during my second hospitalization, my therapist introduced me to the head of the department who knew about OA and eating disorders. I did him a favor and went at his request. I thought, "OK, get off my back, I will go to a meeting." I did. Yet, once again, I did not feel like I belonged or fit in. Most of the people were overweight and I was skinny thin. But when I heard people open their mouths and share about their crazy thoughts and behavior related to food, I thought, "Thank G-d, I am not alone!"

For the first time in my life, I did not have to hide anymore. I had people I could talk to about my relationship with food and how I really felt. It was great! I could go to _A and be with my _A buddies and just be. Eventually, two other bulimics joined my home group and we formed a small subgroup in which I learned I did not have to isolate and be alone anymore. To some degree this carried over into my social life, lessening my feelings of isolation and not belonging. Even with all of these positives, I could not get abstinent for a very long time and still suffered from severe depression.

Eventually, I gave up sugar. However, my disease had progressed, so, that alone did not solve my problem. I saw an eating disorder therapist, who encouraged me to eat small amounts of all kinds of food. I felt like a failure because I was unable to follow her instructions. Today I understand why. I am a sugar/food addict. I cannot have any, not even small amounts of sugar and other trigger foods.

By the Grace of G-d, I met a woman from the United States who had come to do a workshop where I live. We became friends and she arranged for me to get into a treatment program in the States. This was a miracle. For in the country I lived, the only treatment option available was admission to a psychiatric ward. Deep down in my inner being, I knew this was not the solution for me and yet I did not know what the solution was. I kept thinking, "I can't go on like this. I don't really want to die. I'm going to commit suicide because I can't live like this any longer, etc." As difficult as my life was, I knew in my heart I did not really want to die!

I entered an eight-week treatment program and stayed for nine. I know today it is what saved my life. There, I knew what I had to do, but was not fully willing to do it. I was argumentative wanting to do it my way. The staff would just look at me and say, "This is our program and if you don't like it you can get on a plane and go back home." It was like, "Oh my G-d, they really mean business." For me, treatment was a slow and painful process. I had so much fear around eating and exercise. I believed if I started eating and did not throw up, I was going to gain weight and become the size of an elephant. I also believed without regular exercise the same thing would happen. Every morning I fought tooth and nail with the staff to go for a walk. It was denied. I would argue and say, "Exercise is healthy; it is important to prevent osteoporosis, etc." I was never able to admit, I had to go and burn calories to keep my weight down. In reality, I did gain a little bit of weight but not much. Then, I did not think I was manipulative. But looking back now in my recovery, I know I wanted to be in control and to get my way.

Slowly but surely in treatment, I realized something was working. Maybe I should stop kicking and screaming and give up the fight! Accepting the fact I was a sugar and food addict changed the way I looked at the disease and recovery. As the Big Book of Alcoholics Anonymous states, "Acceptance is the answer to all of my problems today."

The thought of being released from the treatment facility was terrifying. I felt safe and protected for I only had to deal with the food during meals and that was always with guidance and support. I could have signed on for life! There I made one of the hardest decisions of my life. Knowing I had to hold onto this little bit of recovery I had gained, I chose to stay in the States for a while. I had to go to any lengths and literally give up everything that I had worked so hard for at home—my family, my nephew whom I adored, my cat, school, work, and more. For me it was life or death and I knew I did not want to die. As painful as it was, I chose to take care of myself and get my priorities right, so I stayed.

Leaving the treatment center, I continued to attend _A meetings and work with therapists, choosing to try all different types of therapy. With this combination of help, I slowly started to put more and more days together without throwing up or overeating. I continued to stay off of my known trigger foods. Because my system was so sensitive, as I got clean and stayed clean, I needed to be "even more clean." I learned I had to add many more items to the list. Today, I believe this is the progression of the disease of an addiction. I define myself not just as an eating disordered person but as a sugar and food addict. For if I put certain substances into my body, they cause the phenomenon of craving, which leads to my having to binge. Daily, from minute to minute, and hour to hour, I choose not to eat these foods and hurt myself.

In the treatment center, I was taught that my recovery is my responsibility, nobody else's. I prefer to eat my own prepared food; however, sometimes I will go out to a restaurant. I am not embarrassed to ask how something is made and what the ingredients are. I just say, "I am allergic" because I am. If necessary, I will speak with the chef. My family may be embarrassed but, oh well, I am not. If need be, I will just order water. When I go places, I often pack my food and take it with me. I have an assortment of coolers and ice packs of varying sizes and shapes. When I travel by plane, I carry a note from my doctor that explains my needs for special foods and supplements. If my luggage is drawn aside and searched, I pull out the note as an explanation. Often, it is not a problem to get what I need but I won't take a chance because I know the slightest thing can trip me up. The bottom line is, by taking all of these measures, I know I am taking care of myself.

To me, my recovery is about making choices. My kids say to me "Why can't you eat A, B, or C?" I say, "I can eat whatever I want. I can eat everything and anything. However, today I choose what I eat and don't eat because of how it affects my health and my sanity." About a year and half ago, I had a need to make changes in my food plan. After a few attempts, I found the right person to guide me. I have had to eliminate many of the abstinent foods I love and enjoy, as well as weigh and measure my food. I have to keep it very simple, stay off all my trigger foods, even when my head tells me they are okay. Kicking and screaming I went back to weighing and measuring because my head does not really know what enough is. If I am in my anorexic head, then everything is way too much. If I am in my compulsive overeater's head, then nothing is enough, and I want more and more. The scale gives me parameters that I don't have internally. Eliminating trigger foods and weighing and measuring what I put in my mouth is the prescription to keeping me healthy. Deep down I know what works and what doesn't. Again, it is my choice to follow my plan and to be abstinent or not.

Fortunately, one day at a time, I have been relieved of the insanity of thinking and dreaming about a lot of the food items from my past, e.g. ice cream, cake, chocolate, etc. But sometimes I do think about the abstinent foods I once enjoyed that have been removed from my food plan. When these thoughts arise, I need to use tools to rid myself of them. Some of the tools I use today include being in contact with other food addicts/compulsive eaters or others with whom I feel safe. This might be connecting by phone or attending a meeting. Through prayer and meditation, I am able to connect with my Higher Power, who is always available to me when I ask. And in my head, I sometimes "run the video" of what my life used to be like when I was eating and bingeing and throwing up without any control. This helps me to see where indulgence in my trigger foods would take me. I DO NOT WANT TO GO BACK THERE, NOT FOR A SPLIT SECOND, I NEED TO KEEP MY MEMORY GREEN!!

For me, my support system allows me to let off steam like a pressure cooker. Without this outlet, I might "explode." I might go into a rage or get depressed. And in the worst- case scenario, stuff myself and my brains with food. In the past, if my kids had opened their mouths to me in anger, once upon a time, I would have screamed back. Now I can say, "Please don't talk to me like that. If you want to talk, I will listen, but do not raise your voice to me." If I was in the food, I would not be able to respond this way. I would have raised my voice, raged, and would have ended up in a horrible fight.

Today, I am in a place of greater self-acceptance. Physically, I am not at the magic number I would like to be on the scale. I am about five to six kilograms more. However, all my clothes fit me even though I often think nothing will. Professionally, I believe with all of my heart that I can help other addicts because I understand their pain from the inside out. It is not just about book knowledge. And personally, I have more flexibility, compassion, and acceptance for those around me as well as for myself. At times I can even say, "I like me" more frequently than not!

How do I know I am an addict? It is not just through my history of abusing food. In the past, I have also abused my thyroid medication by taking more, in hopes of increasing my weight loss. Having a family history of osteoporosis, I put myself at risk because a side effect of the drug is a decrease in calcium. My thinking is that of an addict, give me more, I will take more, and more is better! With this in mind, I do not drink alcohol, which is made from sugars, and do not take anything which contains codeine or opiates. I believe in the phenomenon of craving and avoid any and all substances that could initiate the urge to use. In the past, I wanted to stop and could not. Why would I expect that to be different today?

I am very grateful for my recovery and I like to keep my memory green. The way I was going, I should be six feet under. It's painful for me to talk about the way it was but it's important for me to remember because I do not want to go back there. I had one relapse that lasted for five years, five very long years. I don't know if I can pull myself out of another relapse. Today, I believe my life is a gift. People are placed in my life for me to have the opportunity to both give and receive. I have learned to ask for what I need and accept it graciously as well as to say "No" when I cannot give or do anymore. I have learned that having boundaries is not selfish but can be a wonderful thing for my protection. The 12 steps have enriched my life. For me, recovery is finding balance and feeling safe and most importantly facing life on life's terms drug free.

JOURNEY TO CONTENTED ABSTINENCE

Growing up I don't ever remember being in a *normal* sized body. I always remember being the heaviest one in my class. My mom had to take me to the *overweight* section in stores in order to buy clothing. We didn't have much money, so I didn't ever have very much to wear. I remember I was in junior high school when I first went to a weight lost program. To be honest, I don't ever remember not being on a diet and not being concerned about my weight, my body, and my appearance.

I was one of five children. I had three older brothers and one younger. Growing up, I was the only one who was fat and had a weight problem. I remember my favorite relative would always say to me, "What a pretty face you have, if only you would loose weight." At the same time, she would always take me out for lunch at Embers, a fried chicken joint, and top it off with a sundae at Brighams, an ice cream parlor. What a mixed message I got!

I don't believe I came from an extremely dysfunctional family. My mom and dad loved one another and loved the five of us equally. I never felt abused or misused or taunted about my weight or anything else. My parents and my brothers rarely brought the issue up except to be supportive when I was on a diet.

In high school, I was one of three white kids in my homeroom. I was the only Jew and the only one who was fat. I was also an over achiever and made good grades. I had lots of strikes against me. I remember lifting up my desktop one day and finding a paper bag in it with a note. The note said, "Maybe you should use this." Inside the bag was a large can of Arid extra dry deodorant. Talk about feeling like two cents! Thinking about it, I am not surprised because I never showered

or bathed or did laundry and wore my brothers' sweaters which were
the only items that fit me.

I attended college in Boston and lived on campus. Meals were part of
the deal. I can remember eating whatever I wanted and as much as I
wanted. I can also remember ordering take out with my friends late at
night. During the summers, I would lose weight and then gain it all
back when I went back to school. The semesters that I was on co-op,
working in my field of study, I would lose weight and then gain it all
back once again. I can remember especially using the a diet which was
lots of protein and water. I can remember my boss being concerned for
my health because I didn't eat anything else.

After graduating college, I moved to Chicago for my first professional
work experience. I know today this was an attempt at what is known as
a "geographic cure." I was afraid to stay in B. because I thought I would
not be successful in my career. Actually, it turned out to be a blessing
in disguise, but did not realize it until many years later. While at work,
eating lunch, I heard what would become the gateway to the solution
of my weight problem. A colleague, who was a little bitty bit of a thing,
told me she was only a phone call away from help. She told me she was
a compulsive overeater and she went to −A-. I didn't respond to her
comment and had no idea what she was talking about; however, it stuck
in my mind and I never forgot her words. Although I don't remember
her name, I will never forget her and the gift she ultimately gave me.

When I moved back home, I lived with my parents for a while and
worked nearby. Yet once again, I so wanted to lose weight. I decided
to join a clinic to help me loose weight, which was a 500 calorie/day
program consisting of protein and vegetables. I remember that it cost a
great deal of money. I had to go every day and weigh in and speak to a
counselor. At the time, I didn't drive or have a car, so my mom drove
me. Looking back, that must have been quite a burden to her. I am
not sure I ever expressed my appreciation but would if I could today.
I believe I lost over 70 pounds following the program and dieted my
way into a *normal* size body. In fact, the clinic used a before and after
picture of me in an ad they ran in Canada and the United States. The
ad stated, "...using the skills she's learned Judy knows she won't gain

back the weight she's so proud of having lost." Guess what? Eventually, I gained it all back and more.

Prior to gaining my weight back, I met my husband and got married. On my wedding day, I believe I weighed 149 pounds for a split second of my life. However, it was very short lived for I ate my way through my honeymoon and back. My weight continued to be a challenge. I was always on some kind of diet, whether it was any of the diets or programs, or any other fad diet that came out in a book or a magazine. If I lost weight, then I always gained it back and more. I was what one would call a Yo-Yo dieter. However, I can't imagine what I would have weighed without dieting! Today, I often say, "I would have been 1000 pounds or dead!" I believe that would have been my truth.

My husband and I were blessed with two children. My life revolved around taking care of them, working, managing the house, and of course the never-ending saga of dieting. In early 1990, I started New Direction, a liquid food plan located at a nearby hospital. I had to show up twice a week and get weighed in, have blood work drawn weekly, and attend a group run by a psychologist. I remember them taking a picture of me in front of a grid hung on the wall. At my initial weigh in, the scale read 288 pounds, the highest weight I can ever remember. It was at least 20 pounds more than I had weighed at the height of my pregnancies. Initially, I did well; however, eventually I faltered. The nurse, who weighed me in, said, "Your weight in not a moral issue. It does not mean that you are a good or a bad person. Maybe you are a compulsive overeater. Maybe _A would help you. Maybe you should check it out."

Again, I didn't understand exactly what she had said; however, her remarks triggered me to remember the conversation I had with my colleague 15 years before in a C. cafeteria.

A few weeks later (still on the liquid plan), under the pretense of buying winter hats and gloves for my children, I went to a department store. I proceeded to buy bags and boxes of food items and then headed off to Friendly's for some ice cream. At home, I proceeded to eat it all. I was beside myself with shame and remorse. I had no idea what was wrong with me and how to stop eating. I found the telephone directory and looked up _A and found a number for their *hot line*. I made the call, found a beginners' meeting to attend, and have never turned back.

Has my road of recovery been straight forward without faltering? Absolutely not! I got a sponsor, called my food in to her daily, and followed her directions. I was blessed with abstinence right away, free from sugar and white flour. At least three times a week, I attended meetings; daily read _A and _A literature; made phone calls; and performed service by sponsoring, leading meetings, and booking speakers. Physically, I lost over 100 pounds, got into a *normal* size body, and kept my weight off for a few years. By working the steps from the *steps,* I began to change emotionally and spiritually. I lived with far less fear, I began to like and trust in myself, and I was more present for my spouse and my children. Overall, I was a much happier human being.

One fateful day, I ate a cheese curl that was not on my food plan and it had not been committed. One led to two, and two led to three, and then all bets were off. I took an 80-pound bite. I could not stop eating. I continued going to meetings and continued to call a sponsor. I never left _A, even when I ate before a meeting and after a meeting. I knew I needed the support of a group of like-minded people and a 12 Step program. Nothing else had ever worked for me before. I tried different _A groups in Medford and Chelsea in the Boston area. I just could not stop eating. I did not know what I did not know, and little did I know what was in store for me next.

At a meeting, I met an old friend, who I had previously stepped up in _A. She was radiant, looked absolutely beautiful, and had lost a lot of weight. She told me she was doing a different 12 Step program separate from before, weighing and measuring her food without exception, and not eating any sugar, grains, flour, or starches. I told her I couldn't imagine weighing and measuring my food without exception. She said she understood. I hemmed, and I hawed. However, I could not get the "glow" she radiated out of mind. She truly appeared to be a different person than I had once known—physically, emotionally, and spiritually.

In March of 2004, I joined her 12 Step program and found a sponsor. I struggled with lots of 'Day Ones.' I just could not get it. I did not have the willingness to surrender to the food plan. My attitude was, "Maybe I will be abstinent today?" On April 29, 2005, I ate throughout the day looking for the elusive taste. Did I want sweet or salty? Did I want to munch and crunch? Did I want mush and gush? I did not have a clue. All I do know is on April 30, 2005, my attitude changed. It went from, "Maybe I will be abstinent?" to "How was I going to stay abstinent?" I believe this was a gift from my Higher Power (HP), whom I choose to call GD and fortunately, I have never had to look back. It is why I tell people who are struggling, "Don't keep coming back. Just stick around because you never know when the miracle will happen!"

Today, I am free from the obsession of food. By eliminating all sugar, flour, grains, and starches, I do not have the cravings which used to drive me to overeat and binge. By weighing and measuring my food without exception, I know I have had enough to eat. For whatever reason, I am a person who always wanted more and never felt satisfied. Even today at the end of each meal, I always want more; however, if I wait 10-20 minutes, I am satisfied and can go for four to six hours without thinking of food or eating again. Today, I never feel deprived for I am not on a diet. I am on a food plan that works for me. I know there is always another meal coming. By the way, I consider myself a *foodie*. I love to cook, I love to feed people, and I love to eat good food that is tasty. Today and every day I get to do this guilt free while living in a *normal* size body!

I believe I am a walking miracle! I am maintaining over a 110-pound weight loss for over 12 years. I take care of myself today and think I am worth it. I exercise at least five times a week, I brush and floss my teeth daily, shower, wear clean clothes, laugh, and have fun. When I see my physician, who has known me for over 30 years, he marvels at my blood work, blood pressure, heart rate, and general physical health. I am a kinder, more loving, and less controlling person than I ever was. I can more readily speak up for myself and ask for what I need and not be the door mat I was before, letting others walk all over me. I have open, loving, and honest relationships with my spouse and children. Is it always perfect? Absolutely not! However, I consider myself a work in progress.

Prior to program, my religious mentor suggested that I become a Bar and Bat Mitzvah teacher. I laughed at the idea and thought, "I could never do that!" With program, I gained the confidence and now teach both children and adults and love it. This past year, at the age of 65, I took classes and became one of the first 15 Certified Food Addiction Counselors in the world. Who would have ever thought I would do that! I really did not know what I did not know. I did not know that I could not eat grains of any type and that I have to weigh and measure my food without exception. I am a Food Addict through and through. My body acts as a distillery to these products and sets up a dependency to these foods just like alcohol does to an alcoholic. I am so grateful to know and understand this, for I never have to go back to the misery in which I lived before. Today I live with contented abstinence!

So, let me start at the beginning when I was a skinny kid at about five years old. Although friendly and shy, I met people easily. I was the kind of person that people teased a lot. I was able to eat anything I wanted, and all I had to do was take it. Something about sneaking it appealed to me. I had dyslexia, so I had a learning disability, making me an even bigger target. I stole money to buy sweets or other stuff, and I got a little chubby and then fought everyone. While in this process I was teaching myself not to like me. Of course, I was angry at myself and the whole world as well. So that led me down the road to alcohol when I was eight and drugs when I was ten. I was angry at everyone but mostly at myself. I had a hard time in grade school and got kicked out of high school in my Freshman year. And still, I used everything not understanding what was going on with me or why. I did not like myself or the world around me.

I had a hard time in relationships with girls, and I struggled to figure out my place in the world. I got sober and off drugs the first time when I was 25 and then again when I was 28. This time it stuck, and I have been clean and serene for 36 years. That's when my true addiction showed up, and I ate whatever I wanted and whatever I wanted. I was about 250 lbs. when I came into recovery and ate my up to 400 plus three times in my life. I still struggle with relationships today, but I have a lot of friends and meet people very easily. I have been in many diet programs and picked up diabetes along the way. I struggled with relationships my whole life. What I was doing or supposed to be doing. You know there is not a book to read or a class to take. I probably would not have taken it anyway. But I have learned something in my new abstinence that I am learning how to be happier with just plain old me and that being by myself is ok. It takes a lot of work to find peace in between your meals and then peace between your ears. It's Spiritual in nature and Grace to help you deal with everything else.

I have been a diabetic for over 15 years. In the beginning I ate everything I wanted and could not control my numbers. I was taking several different medications, and nothing was working. I tried several programs, and I struggled with all of them. I have had several nutritionists as well. I have met a dietitian I can now work with. I also have the willingness to listen to what I am told and do what is suggested. It took me a long time. You see I am very stubborn. And I always want things my way. To learn how to meet in the middle, took a lot of 12 step work, a lot of prayer, a lot of writing, and a whole bunch of willingness and trust for me to even learn what was so generously being shared with me.

I have been over 400 lbs. three times in my life and I have been almost 400 lbs. a few times as well. I have also had diabetic numbers between 400 and 600 for a year and did not stroke, and I am and still here to talk about it.

Today it's been almost 16 years I am a diabetic and I now weigh 185 lbs. I am not taking any medicine at this time and have not had any medicine in almost 6 years. My numbers run between 80 and a 100, I eat very well, but it is what is recommended to me by a dietitian and a food sponsor.

I am truly amazed I can do this by just changing my diet! I also have peace in between my meals. My thinking of myself and others has changed, since I have worked the 12 Steps and discarde over 186 lbs., and along with the help of a God of my understanding, a couple of sponsors, a dietitian, family, and some loving and caring friends.

I am Grateful for the love of a Higher Power. And the ability to plan and prepare my meals ahead of time. So, I am not hungry on the run. I know where my next meal is coming from and it makes a difference in the way I feel in most situations.

Thanks for the privilege to be able to share my story.

Abstinent for the last 16 years

My name is ... and I'm overeater and food addict. What does that mean?

Sixteen years ago, I was in a bad place. Physically I was 100 pounds overweight with painful inflammation and stiffness in all joints, and I had a discus prolapse in 3 areas of my spine. I could not get things from the floor. If I dropped something, I had to get a shovel to get it. I could not exercise or go for a walk because of my pain and extra fat. My gastrointestinal tract did not work in a healthy way because my stomach and diaphragm were worn out after years of overeating. I had heartburn and heart rate irregularities, and I had destroyed nearly all my teeth, not taking care of them. Now I am just talking about the physical symptoms that were upsetting or bothering me.

Mentally, I was very weak, sick, sad, depressed, crying, felt like a victim, and I was unhappy. With no self-confidence, I had no strength to do anything for myself or my three kids. Breaking down in tears of loneliness many times a week, I just wanted to be left alone so I could eat my fix or die. Nothing mattered, and I did not want to live the life I was living. Spiritually I was broken down after years of struggle with the weight. I had no control over the food. I was eating one meal a day that lasted from the time I woke up until late in the night. I would fall asleep in a blackout on the sofa. Most of the time, I was in a vicious circle which I had no control over. I had no sense of how much or little I should eat and could not recognize if I was eating too much or too little. I ate even though I was not hungry, and I could not swallow another bit, and while I was sick. I was always trying to take control over my food and had irrational thinking about what would be best to eat. When I had the strength to try something new, I was trying all kind of diets, health-foods, and exercise. I talked to myself saying, "I did not eat so much yesterday, so it is ok to eat today," or, "Yesterday I was eating so much, so I can just eat today and start my diet next Monday." If I did not eat, I was a winner because I had control over my eating, but the minute I let something in my mouth, I lost control and just ate and ate and could not stop. No matter what I tried, nothing ever worked.

The scale would control my eating living like this. I always weighed myself in the morning, in the evening, before and after meals, and before and after bathroom. I ate if I lost some grams/kilos because I was a winner and could afford it. When I did not lose any grams/kilos, I would just eat and start my diet on Monday or after Christmas or after the summer holiday. I am a strong Icelandic Viking woman and have done many things in my life that many others could not do. I raised, mostly alone, my three children, working fulltime hours and while working on my bachelor's degree at the University. However, I could never control my food, and I did not understand why. Every night I promised myself that tomorrow I would do it, tomorrow I will have control over my eating.

Socially, I isolated myself more and more. I drove to work, the store, and home. If I was invited to a party or something, I would excuse myself and lie that I needed to attend to the children and home. It was difficult for me to communicate, I was often angry or annoyed, and it was not much fun to be around me. I would rather be home, on the couch so that nobody would mess with me, but if I went out among people, for example to an invitation, then I would fix my seat near the food, so nobody could see how many trips I would take to get more food. I would excuse myself and say that I had not eaten all day because of work. I was not talking to people nor would I hear what guests were talking about. I was in the food and could not hear or see properly. It was like I was in coma because I was so busy eating and trying to hide the food I was eating. Sometimes I went to a party and ate before to have control over what I would eat at the party. I ate little or what looked "just normal" at the party, but then I went home or to the store to buy more food on my way home. Endless distress, anarchy, and dishonesty characterized my life when it came to food. I had no money because I spent it all on food and candy. But enough was enough.

What happened 16 years ago is that I went to a meeting and got help. I got an assistant who gave me instructions and support to follow a diet plan and a plan that helped me get out of the vicious circle. It was a plan that included my meals, my life, and myself. I got this frame around the food, taking out the food types that caused my addiction to foods I would eat and could not stop once I had started eating them, and I began to recover slowly. Kilograms went off one by one, and the recovery process made my obsession with food to disappear. It disappeared in a few days, and before where there were stupid thoughts about food, I had time for life, my children, and family. The addiction had slowed down by not eating the foods I previously had chosen almost exclusively.

I took out sugar, flour, starch and some fruit. I eat three weight meals a day and nothing between meals. This simple thing has given me new life. Genius and a Miracle! Something happened, and I had no way of doing it without this kind of help and support. I'm still at that place; I cannot do this alone, if I could, I would have done this many years before. Do I know how this work now after 13 years? I do! Why do I need this support and help every day? It is all about the food I was eating, which caused me the inability to stop when I started and it's all about being honest when it comes to food. Everything is on the table, and I am not eating over shame or dishonesty. To give up and ask for help and do this with support is the best thing I have done in my whole life.

Once I was eating at a restaurant in a very prestigious and stylish 5-Star hotel. The waiters were ninety and hundred years old, had worked there all their life, and truly knew how to serve people. It was a pleasure to watch them work. We were referred to the seat and offered champagne while we were deciding what we wanted to eat. I refused the wine, but my boyfriend accepted it, the waiter then asked what I wanted instead, and I was quick and ask for a diet soda. I realized immediately that maybe it would have been better to ask for mineral water, but this fantastic servant said, "Aah, the champagne of America." He smiled like the sun, and he brought me a cold and sparkling diet soda, and I felt just like a princess, with the best drink I could think of.

These waiters spoke another language, and their English was not great, but if there was anything they did not understand, they just called a younger waiter over to translate. I had my needs when it came to food, I weighed it, and got all the services I needed. It is great to be able to be abstinent all around the world as well as in my own kitchen.

Sitting there in that beautiful old hotel was just amazing, and I will never forget that evening with my boyfriend. We had an extraordinary time. That evening became very precious because two days later my boyfriend died, drowning in a river. I lost my boyfriend in the accident, but I didn't have to eat over my feelings. I could cry and laugh and eat my three meals all in one abstinent day.

Yes, I know how this works and what I do and is it just to be thin? To survive, I need this because I am a sick food addict. If I do not take care and avoid the foods that cause me to overeat, I will die. I was nearly there, and I don't want to be there again. I know how life was, because I remember it so well. I was alive but felt dead inside because I had no hope. My soul was dying inside my body. Today I can do whatever I like. I have many grandchildren and can sit on the floor and play with them. I have a new life; I ride a bike to my work, I can walk in the mountains, and I am a fly fisher in big difficult rivers. In my abstinent life, I experience all of life, good and bad!

I have a boyfriend now who loves me and a scale that goes with me everywhere, even on our first date. The scale is my best friend, as it tells me when I have eaten enough and makes sure I'm getting enough to eat. Genius and a miracle.

I need these devices and the help that I am referring to; the organization, the 12 steps, the sponsor, the food plan, the scale and not to say the least, a higher power. I just do this one day at a time to stay alive and stay at peace with myself and the food.

Willingness

How do I become aware of the need for change in my life? How do I become willing to make a change in my life? How do I sustain a change in my life? What resources do I need to make changes? Who do I trust to share my goals and aspirations? These and other questions may be the precursors to successful interventions. Do I trust myself to hold to my commitment to change? Do I need others to support the changes that I hope to make? What kind of commitment do I require to alter, in baby steps, the direction that my life is taking now?

One of my friends once told me that by committing my food each day, one day at a time, that I was making a covenant with her, with God, and with myself. This was a weighty statement. She was a spiritual advisor as well as a friend of many years. Her way of thinking about food and my commitment to a new way of eating, and consequently to a new way of living, helped me to see the change in a spiritual way.

The heart knocks that I've taken over the years to avoid these kinds of commitments and spiritual changes brought me to the point where I considered suicide. Death was the best alternative to a change this grand and demanding. In that solitary moment of decision, I have hovered between past and future. The past had become intolerable and the future, while unknown, was filled with insurmountable fears and darkness. I did get out of bed. I did go to a place where there were other people. I did ask for help. I received what I believe was divine intervention with the support that I was given. That day was the end of the previous life. That day was the first day of the rest of my life. Since that day I have not intentionally eaten any grain or sugar.

I had previously had other experiences of change: the day that I heard the dentist tell me that I would lose my teeth if I did not start to floss each day, and I started to floss that day. I have done so each day since except for one night I went to sleep and awakened in the morning without having flossed my teeth. Another example of change was the day I started to cut the plastic holders for soda bottles. I had seen something that spoke of the sea otters and dolphins and their negative interactions with these plastic holders. From that day until this, I snip the plastic holders. When I recently saw the effects of one of the items on the growth of a turtle and its shell, I felt sad, but not guilty.

Do I have other examples of changes? Brushing my teeth, a minimum of twice a day came late in my maturation. Not because my mother had not attempted to instill the process in me, but more attached to my reticence to do anything every day, much less twice a day. I couldn't imagine, eating three times a day with nothing in between but beverages. An insurmountable task. I was willing to commit one meal. The next morning, I was free from the foggy brain, the aching joints in all parts of my body, and the suicidal depression that had nearly taken my life day before. Miracle? Perhaps. Certainly, grace and achievable/receivable by anyone.

So how to get from here to there? On a mountain slope, the way is either across or down: the skier's choice. You might ask, "What has that got to do with me? I don't ski." I learned how to ski when I was in ninth grade. I learned to ski on powder snow. I didn't know that there was any other way to ski. Then we moved to a desert. The ski slopes in nearby mountains were significantly different from those I had known. Icy, slanted differently, and unforgiving, the slopes there never engaged me. I learned to tack back and forth, fearful of going too quickly down the hill. It was only years later when a ski instructor explained to me that I was "doing it backwards," I learned to do what had been counterintuitive for about half a century. Quite simply I learned from him (having slept on his message) I needed to drop the uphill shoulder, when I wanted to make a turn, and I could alternate the shoulders as rapidly as I recognized which was uphill. Suddenly I could make S turns down the hill while staying secure in the speed and transitions.

Interestingly, this is pretty much the same story with the food. I had tried for my entire life, up to 52 years of age, to moderate my consumption of various food items, to limit my desire to eat, to eat with greater frequency, to curb the changes in my blood sugar with small but frequent meals, to exercise more, to count calories, to deal with my emotional triggers, and to find ways in which to do what I wanted to do with food while obtaining a body I wanted to live in. I was unsuccessful for 52 years. That one meal committed without grain or sugar and with amounts (might I say substantial amounts) was the beginning of a new life like the one on the skis.

That is now 21 years ago, and I live in the body that is 90 to 100 pounds slimmer than it used to be. I live with a head that is surprisingly fog free most of the time. My body, while now 73 years old, is free from aches and pains and arthritis. My lungs, once plagued with asthmatic breathing problems, are now free (except rare times in which I have a diminished immune reaction and need to use inhalers for a few days). These days the inhalers are an exception rather than the rule that they once were. I am free from the 'phenomenon of craving,' and unless I inadvertently take in something that has grain or sugar in it, I continue to be free of the phenomenon of craving each day.

Can you have this experience? I believe the answer is an unequivocal yes.

B.'S STORY

I struggled with falling asleep after lunch each day. I finally realized what I ate was having an effect, a negative one. I had already quit drinking alcohol years before, but sweets were a daily part of my life. When I stopped the daily consumption of the sweets, I no longer fell asleep after lunch!

In 1992 after many incidents of dizziness and blurred vision, which quickly disappeared, I went to a doctor when my symptoms did not go away. My blood pressure was 240/120. He prescribed blood pressure medication, which was changed several times as my pressure kept spiking. He could not regulate my pressure and told me to take pressure pills whenever spikings occurred as he said he could not help me.

For nine years these spikings became more frequent and severe which required more pills to stop the sudden numbness and weakness, sudden confusion and trouble speaking, sudden trouble seeing, sudden trouble walking with dizziness and loss of balance.

Then after heat exhaustion and blood pressure spiking, I went to a local ospital. I had taken about 30 pills before my pressure came down and my heartbeat returned to normal! They asked me why I wanted to commit suicide. I told the interviewer I did it to save my life! I told my hospital doctor about my reaction. Okay one minute and the next minute my heart would beat so hard I had trouble breathing. He agreed with me when I said it was like an allergic response. He told me to take two antihistamines when that happened.

I have kept careful records of what I eat and my reactions. This has changed my life and saved my life.

My blood pressure spikes are triggered by the following:

1. Wax coatings on fruits and vegetables (cucumbers, rutabagas, some squashes, apples etc)
2. Food dyes
3. Caffeine
4. Potatoes washed in a chemical to discourage sprouting)
5. Nuts (pre-cracked) processed in fungicides
6. Epinephrine
7. Eggs washed in liquids other than plain water

Are people allergic to eggs? Or to what the egg is washed in?

Fallacy: washing or cutting wax off vegetables does not remove the was as the liquid portion goes into the product! Plus, it may seal in pesticides and fungicides

Sugar for me causes aches, pains, stiffness, brain fog, extreme hunger, bad flatulence

Veggies grown in dyed water may include broccoli, leafy vegetables, and string beans

Sodium benzoate causes sleep deprivation for me, and sodium benzoate and potassium sorbate are used in liquid vitamins and in some antihistamines.

Polyethylene in some vitamin B 12 causes hives and diarrhea for me

Glycol causes for me extreme body shaking in cold extremities and loss of bowels

Bactrim, Sulfamethorozele, Epi, polyethylene glycol, vitamin E, citric acid: Please read the information as it might apply to you!

Some brands of applesauce are problems for me

The coloring agent for some strawberry yogurt challenges my system

BPA and can linings too

Some vanilla flavorings are derived from anal secretions of beavers and these are problems for me.

I live a life with abstinence from many specific items. As a result, I am alive and heave been healthy enough to enjoy my life dancing the nights away, traveling, playing pickle ball, and trying to share these experiences with others who might wish to live instead of dying from commonly experienced chemicals.

Your particular items may be different from mine, but careful journaling of symptoms and recording what I put into my body (vitamins, food, supplements, beverages) or on my body (lotions, creams, hair products) I have saved my life to LIVE and you may do the same.

Abstinence from harmful items is an individual choice and responsibility. I am 93.

THE HARD ROAD TO GRATITUDE

I have suffered from poor self-esteem for many decades. It has led me to suffer from anxiety and depression for most of my adult life. I believe that my issues began from my childhood. I come from two loving immigrant parents. My father worked 12-hour days and was out of the house before I woke up and returned after my bedtime. He worked seven days a week to provide for his family, so we were never without what was needed. My mother worked hard looking after the house and three challenging children. In her spare time, she helped with my dad's business.

I had strong parental guidance, the best way my parents could do while meeting the family's financial needs. Being from an immigrant family provided its challenges. Plus, I was a chubby child, and this led me feeling different from the other children in school. Often, I received physical and emotional abuse from other children or strangers. Some people thought I did not know that I was a fat kid, so they constantly reminded me. This type of verbal abuse and public ridicule still happens to me today. That hurt a lot and contributed to me feeling so different and worthless.

I also experienced some other childhood trauma that I buried for many years. I learned at an early age that food could provide comfort. Combinations of fat and sugar, fat and salt, sugar and salt, and best of all sugar, fat, and salt worked best. Also, to get some attention or to fit in I used humor. I was always the class clown in school. I used humor as a distraction to attempt to hide my large appearance and to make fun of myself first so that people were laughing with me and not at me. This seemed to be a better option than fighting everyone who made fun of me. Unfortunately, I still use all these coping mechanisms in my adulthood.

When I entered my first year at University, I was majorly depressed. I started having flashbacks of my childhood in my dreams. Nothing I did during the daytime could stop my nightmares. With my nightmares, in combination with my depression, suicide seemed like my only way to stop the pain. A friend found me on the floor passed out and got me medical attention. The irony of that event was evident the following year when my friend committed suicide. Unlike for me, no one was around to save her.

My desire to harm myself did not leave me after my first attempt at self-harm. My pain and feelings of shame, guilt, fear, and anger were with me daily. I learned to use food to punish or cause self-harm. I woke up the next day happy if I had a headache, was dizzy or nauseous to the point of throwing up or had feelings of self-hatred. In some mentally twisted way, I felt I deserved whatever negative symptoms I got from eating garbage. This could have been due to my feelings of worthlessness, not lovable, or the combination of the two. Food could be used to numb, sooth, comfort, and as a weapon.

Fast forward about five years, and I was at another university with the same problem. Now I was over 500 lbs. and majorly depressed again. I was also in love with an unattainable woman. She provided me great friendship and support, and I thought I could not be without her. With my enormous weight, depression, and a broken heart the pain was once again unbearable. Again, I was prepared to kill myself. Thankfully my friend intervened and sent the police to my place, and I lost the will of attempting to harm myself again for now.

After that intervention I began to get some emotional help. Because I started to feel better about myself, I started a weight loss program that helped me lose about 200 lbs. over 18 months. I was so motivated that I went for a professional degree. However, being removed from my home environment and a regular routine, I began coping with the stress of college life by overeating again. Once again, I confused a women's help, support, and friendship with love. Once again, I felt like killing myself. Instead, I ate excessively to numb my thoughts or to punish myself for falling in love. Even though I never felt worthy of someone else's love or affections I still felt love towards others. I knew if I told someone how I felt about them I would lose their friendship. That was something I was never willing to risk. Plus, how could someone like me be loved? These thoughts of worthlessness and unlovable gave me significant anxiety and depression. I often suffered panic attacks to the point of passing out because I was unable to control my thoughts. Once again, I quickly managed to get myself well over 400 lbs. When I graduated, I was at about 450lbs. I knew what weight loss program worked before, so I went back.

Now back down to 250 lbs life felt great. I had my third university degree, was employed, and in the best shape of my life since I was 16 years old. Soon after, I got married to a wonderful woman. It was the first time that I ever felt truly loved. I was loved for who I was, and this was challenging to a person with low self-esteem like myself. Wondering if I deserved another person's love my weight slowly began to creep its way back up to over 400 lbs. again. After trying so many weight loss programs without lasting success, I thought I needed surgical intervention. I decided to get the lap band surgery. Sure, the weight began to come off, but I was miserable. I was not always able to keep my food down. The band became tighter when I was stressed or anxious. This made eating solid food, at times, impossible. I was afraid to do anything about the band since my weight gains were under some control.

I was blessed with a true gift and miracle when my wife became pregnant with our first child. Things could not be happier for my wife and me at this time. However, midway through my wife's pregnancy, she developed some troublesome symptoms. Unfortunately, after numerous doctor and hospital visits my wife's health issue was unknown. At her 33rd week of pregnancy, doctors believed she had cancer. Our child needed to be delivered early so my wife could get further diagnosed and treated. Once our son was born, it was determined that my wife had a rare form of lung cancer. It did not take too long after her diagnosis for her to succumb to her cancer.

I was left to deal with my wife's loss and raise our miracle child alone. It did not take me too long to get my anxiety and depression back again, and my weight climbed up again as well. Once again, I was using food for comfort or punishment. I had a high degree of difficulty dealing with my reality. After receiving some medical treatment for my low mood, I began another attempt at my weight loss. Down over 100 lbs. I started to feel great again. I was functioning at work and in my home life much better. However, once again life became stressful. Once again, I went to my old familiar habits of medicating or harming myself with excessive amounts of the worst possible foods. By this point, my binging on food became my daily ritual. However, I still had my lap band, so there were many days I could not keep my food down.

A few years ago, I had all I could take from my lap band, so I had it removed. During the surgery, I experienced some complications and was told I was about ten heartbeats away from death. My immediate reaction was I missed a great opportunity to end my pain. Now I was in real trouble because nothing could stop me from eating copious amounts of food. The dam was broken, and my mouth was wide open. Going to work became nearly impossible. Getting older and getting heavier was not great on my joints. Additionally, the amounts of food I was eating led me to feel so hungover I could not go to work. It also made it impossible to care for myself nor my child.

One day I was so ill at work I collapsed. I was admitted to the hospital with a suspected pulmonary embolism. After about ten days of investigation and medical testing, nothing was found. It was believed that my symptoms were merely a result of my anxiety and stress. When I was released from the hospital, I knew I had a massive problem with my mood and food. I believed my mood problem was a direct result of the severity of my food addiction. I needed help, but I just did not know where to turn. With the help of a friend and leader of a healthy eating support group, I was directed to see a therapist that specializes in food addiction. My eventual food addiction therapist recommended that I contact a friend of hers to design a meal plan to treat my obsession with food.

So, I began to speak with this nutritionist that dealt with food addiction. After listening to my story and trigger foods, he designed a food plan. The food plan was tweaked a few times to provide me with the best food peacefulness. I was able to follow his meal plan, for the most part.

However, I would add an extra piece of fruit now and then. I don't believe I was adding the fruit because I was hungry. The meal plan provided me with ample fullness and satisfaction. I would get cravings for sugar at times, and I thought a piece or 2 of fruit would be a harmless option. He also suggested that I go to a daily 12 step meeting for my addiction with food and my spiritual development. Initially, I opted to follow the food plan only. Eventually, I found a meeting that I liked. I thought I could manage my food addiction with a therapist, meal plan, and one meeting a week.

However, I kept relapsing with something sweet like ice cream or with flour like a pizza. Looking back, I think it had a lot to do with the lack of regular meetings and too much fruit in my diet that behaved like sugar in my addictive brain. Whenever I would get stressed, I would go back to medicating with food. Without the spirituality, fellowship, and support from attending a regular 12 step meeting, along with my sugar in the excess fruit I was eating, I had no chance. My stressors led me back to medicating my feelings and emotions with food. I kept restarting my abstinent meal plan but with no lasting effects.

Every year around my son's birthday I felt blessed and reminded of my loss at the same time. This feeling of depression and sadness would extend to the anniversary of her passing, the anniversary of our wedding, and Mother's Day, which was all a week apart. However, this past year was a little different. I became close to another woman. After about six years of grieving my wife's loss, I thought I could get close to another woman as a friend. In a short time after becoming good friends, she found out she had breast cancer. During a surgery that she required, she experienced some complications that led to her death. With my friends passing plus my son's birthday and all those associated strong negative emotions, I went running to my old friend...food. By this time, I was eating to escape from my pain and sadness or punishing myself daily, and was not sleeping, missing work frequently, not being able to care for myself or my son. I would keep my son from school, so I would not be alone. I often fed him takeout and food delivery since it was too difficult to stand on my feet for any length of time. At this point, my family felt they had to intervene to look after my child. They wanted me to work on myself to recover.

Soon after that, I collapsed again at work. My manager at work and I felt I needed to take a lengthy medical leave of absence. Also, at that time I was on the waiting list for an inpatient treatment center for my depression and anxiety. It took several weeks for me to get admitted. In that time, I reached a new rock bottom. Being over 500 lbs. again, no job, my son not in my direct care, no mobility but with plenty of time to think and eat. I was harming myself to end the pain. I would pass out for a while and recover and soon after I would try to hurt myself again only ending up passed out longer, but eventually recovering. This pattern would continue until I finally got admitted for treatment.

I spent 56 days in treatment for my mood and anxiety problems. The program brought up a lot of intense emotions. Food was not enough to numb my thoughts and feelings. I turned to drinking alcohol as well. I used to drink heavily in my college days, and for the most part, I stopped once I was out of school. I began drinking heavily again while in treatment for my mood and anxiety. Now I was addicted to alcohol and food, so my addiction to sugar now extended to alcoholism. However, upon discharge from the treatment, I learned many useful tools to manage life stresses one moment at a time. The most amazing gift I received was HOPE. I also learned that my feelings of worthlessness and not deserving of love were decisions I made about myself as a child. In a sense, I could recreate who I am by my daily actions and not by what I decided I was as a scared child. I knew that my lasting mental recovery was dependent on me applying the tools I learned daily and getting the support that I so desperately needed.

Before I left treatment, I planned to meet up with doctors and therapist I required for recovery. I put the greatest emphasis on recovery from my food and alcohol addictions. I reconnected with my previous food addiction therapist for help. I was recommended to see a woman who runs a food addiction seminar and retreat. I immediately registered for the retreat and weekly food addiction seminar. I also remembered the meal plan given to me by my food addiction nutritionist which provided me with peaceful meals when I followed it. I remembered that an extra piece or two of fruit was a trigger for me especially if the fruit was in the evening or near my bedtime. I also recalled what Dave emphasized which was the only way to give my recovery with food and now alcohol addiction a chance is to do a daily 12 step meeting for a minimum of 3 months.

For the first time, I felt motivated to deal with my mental wellness, including depression and anxiety, along with my addictions, and managing my physical wellness better. My most significant motivator was getting my son back. However, I knew I had to make myself a priority and work on my mental and physical health before I even think of getting him back.

For me to find recovery I knew I needed to change the way I did things. First and foremost, I needed to think less and do more. When I got back home from my inpatient treatment I needed to change my home environment. I got rid of the TV in my family room. Living as a bachelor, with my son, I ate on the couch while watching TV and that behavior had to change if I was going to have any chance of recovery. I replaced the TV and the couch with a dining room table. Now when I eat, I can focus on the food that I prepared. If my son is over, we can share our daily stories over a meal. I moved my couches from the family room to the living room to make more of a conversation and comfortable reading room. Also, my bedroom is a place I can meditate, listen to music, read or journal. However, watching mindless TV in my bedroom is no longer an option.

Through my daily 12 step meetings, I have found fellowship, support, spirituality, and foremost, a sense of belonging. To be honest, the first couple of weeks of my removal of sugar and any flour from my diet was a struggle. Giving up the alcohol was a little bit easier for me for whatever reason. Once my sugar withdrawal subsided, I found I was able to think more clearly. I was able to concentrate better on what I read, saw, or heard. I found out I enjoyed journaling. It was a way to organize my thoughts and better understand what I am feeling.

That is one of my biggest changes. I can be with my feelings and emotions a lot better. I don't need to be numb myself from what I am feeling with food anymore. I finally realized that no one ever died from having intense feelings or emotions. I might feel sad and cry. I might get frustrated and angry. But once I acknowledge my feelings, they usually do not last very long. If I do have a troubling thought, I can communicate that with somebody or journal about it. So far that has worked well for me.

The biggest impact on my recovery from my addictions is probably due to two major issues in my past that I have been able to forgive myself and let go of completely. Through my work in my inpatient treatment, food addiction seminars, 12 step meetings, journaling, and the fellowship I have learned to let go of the two events that have troubled me for a while.

First is regarding my wife's death. As I mentioned around my son's birthday until mid-May, I would be extremely depressed and anxious. The reason is not due to the loss of my wife. My sick mind had convinced me that I was responsible for her death. I thought I could have done things better that could have made a difference. First, I don't have the ability or power to give anyone cancer. Second, I might have done some things differently through the benefit of hindsight, but there is no guarantee that if I did things differently that it would have made a difference. However, it may have been possible that I could have lost both my wife and child. I can second guess myself about many things, but my wife passed away, and I can't change that fact. I was not responsible, and I truly did my best with a very stressful situation.

The other issue was with my childhood trauma. While I was a child, I concluded that because of my trauma I am worthless and unlovable. I might have decided that as a child but then I believed it into my adulthood. It doesn't matter why I chose to medicate my feelings and emotions with food or to use food as a weapon to punish myself. However, I believe it began when I experienced my trauma and what I thought it meant about who I was as a person. I finally realized that I let a child decide who I was: a scared boy, without experience or wisdom. Through journaling, I made peace with the people involved with my trauma. I believe I suffered enough from this issue. It is so freeing to let that pain, fear, anger, sadness, guilt, and shame go after all these years.

Letting go of these two issues in my life has been the best gift I could have ever given myself. The freedom and the peace I feel is complete joy and happiness. It feels like an enormous weight has removed from my shoulders and chest. I have been freed from the shackles of the food and alcohol. I can honestly say I have a better relationship with my food. Food is about providing nourishment and energy in a healthy way. I can now eat to feel satisfied and not full. I know I can't put even a sip of alcohol in my mouth. It's just another form of sugar for me. Letting go of these issues also goes beyond the addictions. I feel happier about who I am, and I have begun the process of self-love, compassion, and acceptance. Also, I realized that my self-love has nothing to do with my reflection in the mirror. I won't wait till I lose my excess weight, or find a companion, or be a millionaire, or whatever to love myself. I love myself today in this moment. I'm not waiting for anything anymore.

My daily 12 step meetings have also provided me with another gift of peace, serenity, and mental clarity. Because of several losses, I have experienced; my friend's suicide, my wife's death and the more recent passing of a close friend, I questioned my purpose. Also, I had several unsuccessful suicide attempts and self-harming moments. I even escaped a near death after the surgery of the removal of my lap band. Why am I still alive and my loved ones gone? I must have some great purpose that I could never possibly live up to. I don't believe my small brain could comprehend or figure out my purpose. However, I am now closer to my spirituality and my higher power. All I need to do is focus on the present, each little moment that makes up my day, and the rest will take care of itself. If I stay abstinent from sugar, alcohol, and flour today, I will be in a better place mentally to handle every day. Doing this will bring me closer to my goals in life, one day at a time. By living my life this way, I am sure I will eventually learn my purpose. Looking too far in the future could feed my anxiety. My past is behind me. I can't change anything that happened to me in the past.

I am very grateful for all the support and fellowship that I have received. I learned that I need help to stay in recovery. Asking for help makes me wise, not weak. I can already see the benefits of my work in recovery from my food addiction. I have a better relationship with my son. I am not raising him from the couch anymore, and I interact with him in a whole new way. I do activities with him, I encourage him, and I relate to him. I have much more patience with him as well.

I know he notices the change in me as well. I have also been offered a new position at my work. It allows me the ability to get used to the working environment slowly. It also allows me the flexibility to keep the meetings and appointments that I require to stay in recovery. I am also thankful for my family. I now have an honest relationship with my family. I am slowly regaining their trust. My family has always loved and supported me, but now I can be a better son and brother to them.

My story was a privilege for me to write for several reasons. I'm not sure if my story is much different to most people who suffer from addictions. I hope that there is something in my story that the reader can relate with and have hope in overcoming the issue. In no way do I mean it would be easy. However, I hope I did a reasonable job explaining the solution. If you suffer from food addiction, a healthy meal plan from a nutritionist that understands food addiction is first and foremost. An addict may know their foods that they cannot limit in any circumstance. However, no addict should design or create their meal plan. Hire a nutritionist experienced in creating a meal plan that provides a feeling of satiety, satisfaction, and peacefulness. Find the support you need that will support and encourage your abstinence. Addiction is a very isolating disease. Do your best to build your community of support and reach out whenever you need them. An easy place to get support and fellowship is by attending a 12-step meeting in your area in person, by phone, or by podcasts. Remember to focus on each 24-hour day. You may need to break your day up in hours. You don't have to give up your addiction forever. That is hard to do, but you just need to give up your addiction today. Then repeat that mentality daily. Remember you can't change your past and your future has not happened yet. Focus on your day one moment at a time. Also, if you suffer from mental illness, like me, please seek professional help cause you're worth it.

I also enjoyed sharing my story with the reader. The act of writing my story was very therapeutic. I got to see my life as a complete picture. I have been through some challenges. I handled each situation the best to my abilities at the time. Maybe I can have a little more compassion, love, and acceptance for myself after taking an honest perspective of my life. I want to offer my gratitude to the authors of this book for asking me to write my story. I hope the reader enjoys my story as much as I did writing it. I am finally on my journey in recovery. I am enjoying each moment and grateful for what I have now. Anything is possible since I found hope.

MY STORY SO FAR

I come from a long battle with food obsession and compulsive eating. I have gained over 100 lbs. three times in my life, and I have lost over 100 lbs. Three times in my life (with lots of intermittent losses/gains of 20-50lbs in between). That's a one-hundred-pound loss for each of the past three decades to be exact; my twenties, thirties, and early forties. I think this means I have a problem that is outside of what the norm is for folks who are just dieting or who have a problem with their weight. I have tried everything and believe that the medical profession, therapy industry, and the general public don't understand what is going on with folks like me. The ones I have gone to for expert help and solutions like doctors, psychologists, counselors, therapists, eating disorders clinics, don't really understand the how to deal with the seriousness of what's going on.

In my teens, I was in an eating disorders clinic twice in my life, once when I was 16 and once when I was 18. Each time, I was admitted because I just could not stop binge eating and was also very depressed because of it. I lost some weight, my family was part of the in-treatment therapy, and then each time I left treatment, I just began living life again, with a diet mentality. I would try the tools I learned in treatment, which were moderation and feeling feelings, but the compulsive eating would just come back. In my 20's I lost the first 100 lbs. by monitoring food intake, calorie counting, and exercising. I did it all on my own with the help of a doctor that I would see once a month to track progress. He wanted me to go on pills to help with appetite suppression, but I refused and went with the calories he suggested which was 1000-1200 per day. I lost that 100lbs in 4 months.

In my late 20s to early 30's my weight went back up and I tried things like eating disorder women's groups and weekly counseling. At 33 I was at a high of 292 lbs and I was so desperate that I went to regular Overeaters Anonymous meeting. I had gone to them before when I was in treatment, and it never worked for me. I always observed that in the meetings I went to, that there was a tiny minority that had a normal sized body. In those meetings, the seriousness of not bingeing, the way I needed to hear it, was nonexistent and there was too much ambiguity around the food. The people I would listen to in those meetings were still playing around with the disease, and I did not hear clarity around abstinence and structure around the food. But, I thought I would try it again since I got to the point that I just cloud not stop eating. I was 32 and desperate and could not go on another day without help. I didn't even put socks on before I left the house, because bending was such a chore at that size.

Thankfully the meeting I did go to was a _A meeting. _A is a 12-step food program that did not eat any sugar, carbs or grains. They weighed and measured everything without exception, even in public, at work, and at people's houses. Everything was about micromanaging the food, writing it down, calling it into a sponsor and going to meetings and living a 12-step life, and creating number 10 meals (making the food really delicious). For the first time, I truly felt that the gnawing compulsion and obsession of the disease had lifted. I was no longer in its prison. The food was in one hand, and I had life in the other and it was beautiful. What mattered most is that for the first time, I felt free.

I lost 130lbs with _A when I was 33/34. I had two whole years away from active addiction. Imagine me a compulsive eater being happy with having two years of freedom. That was so much time, compared to the misery of food all the other years of my life. I was very involved in the community and supplemented by going to _A meetings. I was willing to do anything to not eat. But after two years, I had grown weary of the weighing and measuring without exception and I was not hearing things in the meetings that made weighing and measuring the rest of my life without exception worth it to me. I began focusing on how many folks were showing up chewing gum and drinking diet sodas at excessive rates and talking about their abstinent # 10 meals.

At times, looking forward to my number 10 meals to take the edge off was an obsession that I fell into in _A and that made me feel like I was binging. Because I began to act in a disease way again, around my abstinent meals, I thought it was too close to the disease for me, even though it was protected within my GS abstinence. Compulsive eating, the behavior, is a trigger for me. It can spiral out of control, even in my abstinence. It's a nuance for me that I need to support.

So, I left _A. I felt like I needed something different. When I pulled away from not weighing and measuring my first meal, after two years of doing just that, I felt as if I was a paraplegic getting up from my wheelchair and walking again for the first time. It was an amazing feeling and scary at the same time. I still had the _A recovery that was with me, and it was very strong, but I left the community and found another 12-step group that practiced "going to God" in all things, even the food. They worked the BIG Book to deal with wanting to overeat or binge eat and took others though the steps. These meetings I attended were not live; they were phone calls or Skype sessions. I kept hearing the message of "the scale is a human measure." It says in the Big Book, "no human measure will work." So, I stopped using the scale, and focused on getting through the 12 steps and practiced living in steps 10, 11, and 12. I was doing this with two years of fresh _A recovery still in my system. Slowly I started not to manage my food intake again. In the group I was working with they said I was eating again because I was not doing enough tenth steps or working with others enough. After about six months, I began bingeing again and gaining the weight back. It was a horrendous feeling. The folks I was working with were calling themselves "recovered" compulsive eaters. That's what I desperately wanted, to be recovered from this illness. Here I was, believing that I could be spiritual enough to not have a scale and not have my food on complete lockdown. I can't go to God with my food. For me that like telling an alcoholic, go to God and ask him which alcohol you should drink and how much. It just does not work from someone like me. I wanted freedom but I was in relapse and could not get out. I did not want to be abstinent and still obsessing with abstinent food (weighing and measuring, calling a sponsor, going to meetings, not eating no matter what and without exception, under any and all conditions like in _A), but I wanted freedom from the compulsive eating!

This was a great lesson for me because now I knew I needed more than just "conscious contact with God" in all things. I needed to stay away from certain substances. When they get in my body, I go nuts, and I don't know when it will stop. I need a structure around my food. I need to know that same feeling with the food as when an alcoholic says "I don't drink" and knows that they don't drink. I need to know what that means for me with the food. What is my "I don't eat?" I knew where that clear line was when I was in _A and that clear line gave me a lot of freedom.

So, for the next five years, I began circling like crazy, like a pinball machine. Going to this or that program and trying the various abstinence-based support 12 step groups like _A. In-between my journey in and out of the different 12 step food programs I experimented with different ways of eating. I ate all raw food, doing a raw food boot camp and eating 1200 cal a day with mostly fruit and 10-15 % fat. I tried intermittent fasting (IF), eating only during a 5-hour period and fasting for 19 hours. I tried the vegan plans. I tried a plant based only eating plan. I tried following a juicing program. I was all over the place. Doing these things may help someone who is not a compulsive eater or food addict but for me, I could not sustain consistency.

When I did intermittent fasting I had great success and was amazed at how the weight was coming off. But most importantly, and with a lot of relief, the constant conversation and obsession in my head about food came to a screeching halt. I did IF perfectly for two months, and I thought this is great! My obsession with food was controlled, I felt confidence, got stronger in my ability to not listen to the voices to binge, and felt like my need to binge on food had gone away! This concept of having a window of time to eat and not restrict (weighing and measuring) anything during that time was a relief for someone that had to think about food all day long, within the 12 step food programs.

The truth is that IF may work for "normal" people, whatever that means. But for someone like me, a compulsive eater and food addict, it was only a temporary win and not sustainable long term with all the other support someone like myself requires. Life happened and I needed ease and comfort one day, and I did binge at the end of that

2-month time. I tried to get back to my 5-hour window a few times but then went back to full on binging again. Also, I was eating sugar or flour in my 5-hour period from time to time and I do believe this played a prominent role as they produce uncontrollable cravings that I could not stop. Imagine a big wave coming to the shore from the ocean. Is there any way you can make a wave reverse and go backwards? No human ingenuity can do that. There is no way to make the craving reverse once I have those substances in my body. The craving is there until it's gone and it's only goes away if I take those substances out, detox, and build a life that supports me in not putting those substances back in my body.

So, what I am trying to say is that I have a serious problem. I am not a dieter that just needs to lose some weight. I am not normal around food issues and not sure anyone is but, I don't feel like society talks about this issue in any way that makes any sense. It seems like everyone is confused. I was up to 240 lbs again and need to lose 100 lbs at least. I had a renewed commitment. I also have evidence that I CAN NOT DO THIS ALONE, or virtually only, or through just dieting. I need a community of support coupled with not eating certain substances and to be around people that were serious about living this way. So, I ran back to _A. It was the ONLY thing that had worked in the past, and there I was not able to stand myself anymore. That piece is essential as it propelled me into the acceptance, surrender, and structure of _A abstinence once again. I was abstinent for eight months in _A again. Lost 100 lbs. and was feeling great and then, my mind switched again, in an instant. "I don't need to do this, and I can just return to intermittent fasting and just not eat sugars, starches or grains, on my own. That was 2015.

From 2015 -2017 I was a pinball machine again. I kept my weight within a tight range, meaning I would not gain or lose more than 25 lbs. But I did gain and lose 25 lbs. through many cycles. When I lost control, the weight began to creep up until it reached very close to the 25 lbs. mark. Then I would quickly clasp the food down with either a 12-step food program like _A or _A until I felt "off the sugar" and then I would leave and then jump into a different plan, like keto, paleo, or intermittent fasting again.

This time I tried a program which is a big community of folks that eats ONLY from the animal kingdom, no plant material whatsoever. I did this for four months and found amazing results. I dropped 35 lbs., my constipation was relieved, I had no inflammation in my joints, and I was never hungry. The obsession and compulsion to binge was removed for about two months but then returned. The community that I was in was very supportive to folks like myself and there were a lot of people in that community that were healing all sorts of ailments but also lots of folks with eating disorders and food addictions there. At the end of 4 months, something happened, and I binged and could never get back to eating all meat. I began my usual pattern again of going to various 12 step programs, getting a sponsor, getting clean from the food substances that are addictive to my body: sugar and carbs and then I would leave again and try IF for a while until I started binging again. Then I would return to a 12-step food program and get clean for a little while until I got tired and wanted to try something else. Are you catching on to my mania yet?

Each time I have gotten off the sugar, flour, and grains I have had to create an ICU type environment in my life. I have taken days off of work, canceled all plans and kept my interaction with the outside volatile food environments (work can be a volatile food environment for people like me), and social interactions to a minimum. For at least 5 days of coming off of sugar, flour, and grains I need to be extremely careful and gentle with myself. Anything during that time can plunge me back into the food. This is a serious illness, and when you get to the place in the game where you are far down the scale in terms how badly your brain is addicted and reacts, it needs to be handled with great care. It would have been great, these past years if I could have walked into a halfway house for food addicts and gotten clean for five days or if my doctor wrote me a note for work saying I needed to stay home and detox, but our society is not there yet. However, I think we need to be there soon, with the current epidemic in our midst.

I can say that 2015 through most of 2017, were years where I just kept bouncing around. Getting control, losing it, trying what had worked in the past, losing control again, and stabilizing for some time, all while losing and gaining the same 25 lbs. over through what I would say was about 15 cycles (I have kept evidence of this in journals). I even tried _A, which is a great solid program, but I really can't feel that completely free feeling when I use grains. And as I write this today, at the beginning of 2020 and 45 years of age, I can say that I do have a serious problem; I am a late stage compulsive eater and food addict. The fact that I did not gain 100 lbs again, for the 4th time came only from true grit, a process that is extremely energy draining and filled with a lot of pain and suffering. I know what works for someone like me and have come to accept it as something I need to do for the rest of my life.

I need a structured way of eating that is entirely free of sugar and grains. I need to know and have a precise definition of my abstinence so that my brain knows that what I am doing with my food is not me behaving in a diseased way with the food. I can enjoy my food, but I also need healthy neutrality with it, not a rigid one. I know I am not "in the food or playing with the food." Because I am late stage, this is something I must have in place. I know I can't do this alone and need a vast support network of others who are like me doing what I do. My brain needs to feel that it is part of a tribe or community of folks that are living this way and free from the devastating effects of being in active addiction. I need this community because the second I walk out the door I have family, friends, media, the glamur industry, the exercise industry, the medical profession, the therapy industry, and the food industry giving me other ideas. Ideas like moderation. That does not work for someone like me. You don't see a heroin addict have just a little heroin and still stay clean. You don't see a cocaine addict snorting just a few granules of cocaine, and you don't see an alcoholic sip liquor while managing their alcoholism. No! You don't. Why would it be different for someone like me who ingests sugar or flour and has more light bulbs going off in the brain than heroin, cocaine, and alcohol combined (it has been evidenced in the research). Complete abstinence is required, forever.

The reason why my story is titled "My story so far," is because I don't know what's going to happen next. So far things have stabilized. I do this just for today. I am comfortably and gratefully back in _A. It's the only thing I have ever done that's given me any kind of long term abstinence. The no matter what and without exception principal in this program works for my brain. I know what I can and can't do and I can build my life knowing I am 100% clean and clear with my food. It may be hard to understand that freedom if you have never experienced it, but this program is how I feel free. I will never be normal around food and weight, and I need extensive peer support. Some foods can never knowingly enter my system again. If you feel you may have something like what I have, get into a group you feel good about. No group is perfect. Certain groups may not be "your people." Follow a plan that works for you and the context of your life; there are many to choose from. 12 step groups are not the only groups out there that are supporting people, but they are very convenient, and they have been doing this for many decades now. If you work with a non 12-step group, make sure they have some supports in place for food addicts and compulsive eaters. Don't just rely on virtual support. Your brain is designed to interact with people, not objects. We have not changed much since our caveman and woman days. You need live people that know who you are either in your neighborhood or people that you can see yearly at a convention or retreat. Be honest about who you are. If you are like me, accepting that you have a lifelong illness, like compulsive eating and food addiction, is the only way to turn things around. Accepting this is a gift for yourself and your loved ones.

MY SURGERY FAILED

I lost the weight and got my life back, but it wasn't from the surgery. It wasn't until I was introduced to food addiction and the idea that certain foods were controlling my life, that I could become the person I was meant to be. I was born in Midwest. When I was young, my parents moved to different city. I had three siblings; I was the second oldest. Growing up was tough due to the emotional and physical abuse inflicted on all of us. I got the worst of it, I was also sexually abused. I don't even know who knew.

I can't remember the good times as a child, I know my family was involved in church, and we went camping in the summertime. We would go up North to stay at a campground in a tent. My mom filed for divorce, and my dad had to leave the house. I had mixed emotions. TI don't remember having any friends during the elementary school years. I was always withdrawn and stayed in the house, and I felt different from all my schoolmates.

I was very quiet until junior high. My best friend. and I loved to play the snare drums together. I tried and tried and practiced and practiced but couldn't pick it up. I gave it up, and she stayed with it. L and I didn't hang out after school; we just hung out during school hours. Around the age of 13, I remember joining a drum and bugle corp. They taught us how to play an instrument or to twirl a rifle or a flag. I chose to play the bass drum. In our uniforms we would move around the field to the music being played. The uniforms were very heavy and hot, especially during the summertime. There were times I would pass out. I enjoyed being in the drum corps because we would go to different cities and have a competition against other drum and bugle corps. The fainting concerned the leaders, so much that they asked my mom to take me to the doctors. The doctor performed different tests on me, but they couldn't find a reason for my fainting. I was asked to leave the corps because they were concerned about my health. This upset me because it was one of the only activities I was able to enjoy during that time in my life.

In my third year of junior high, my mom decided to move further away from school. I was forced to switch schools and lost my friendship with a girl. It was difficult to make new friends. At this age, I was more social and outgoing; I started doing things with my friends. Then maybe when I was 15, I got involved with the church. I became involved because they made me feel special and cared about me. I got involved with the church's different outreach programs, their Sunday school, and their youth group. The youth group had a volleyball team, which competed with other teams. The ministers were also supportive of my sister and me, and they cared for us like family.

In my first year of high school I wanted to belong with the other kids, so I never got dressed for gym class. I got in big trouble with my mom, so that didn't last. I got involved with the high school band, and we played at the football games. We even got to travel to go and march in a another city, I remember going, but nothing else stands out in my mind about that experience. I had a dream of attending a religious college. My mom never had money, and I didn't know anything about the different kinds of scholarships or financial aid, so that was a big letdown. My next wish was after I graduated from high school when I wanted to go into the military, and this is what happened.

I passed all the tests and was shipped out for basic training. Basic training was eight weeks long. While in the army you had to meet a specific weight requirement and be physically fit by passing a physical education test which consists of a certain number of pushups, sit-ups, and a two-mile run. I was young and energetic, so I passed easily. The females also had to take a pregnancy test. My pregnancy test came back positive. I tried to fight it, but I lost and was sent home. Once I was home, I saw my doctor for the pregnancy test, and it came back negative. I wanted badly to be in the military, so I reenlisted to different branch. Once again, I was sent to training and again, I had to take the pregnancy test, and it came out positive. This time I fought the results, I explained that this had happened before, and I was not pregnant. I did retake it, and it was negative. I finished basic training. Some of the tasks we had to perform were going into the gas chamber, firing a rifle, throwing a grenade, but the most important was working as a team.

Now basic training was over, and I was on my way to my advanced individual training as a specialist. This training was also eight weeks long. I graduated and went back home. The duty was one weekend a month, and two weeks in the summer. I don't remember where we went for this. I served ten years with I lived at my mom's house with my sister. When not on duty, I worked at a research firm with my mom. The research firm had mice and dogs they used for research. I don't remember how long I worked there, but my job was to clean the cages. While working there, I met my relative. She was the one who introduced me to the man I started dating him, and it wasn't a long time until I ended up in his bedroom, then into his bed, and then, surprise, I was pregnant. Once I found I was pregnant, I felt I must get married. My husband and I got an apartment. He was happy because his mom and sister were five houses away. He was always drinking, and I didn't let it bother me then. I don't even remember if I was drinking along with him. I had my first child, a beautiful baby boy. Things were going well. I had the support of both our families, which made a big difference for us. But after our first child, my husband started to become verbally abusive to our son. Life went on, and I got pregnant again, and I had a beautiful baby girl. The abuse continued with our daughter as well.

At some point, I was starting not to like being married and having kids. I couldn't handle the stress of managing the home and being in a relationship with my husband and our children. I filed a report against my husband for the abuse. They came over to investigate the report, and they had enough evidence to open a case against him. We started to receive service, and this only put more stress in our home. The kids were placed in a foster home. Six months went by, and I wanted my kids back! We would have them for visitation, and I started missing them as soon as they left. We talked and had a treatment plan in place, which if we followed, they would allow our children to come home.

The kids were released them to my husband and me. I used the system on and off for many months until he started to have them monitor me. Well, all hell broke loose. We had to go to counseling to change our ways with each other and to stop taking our anger out on the kids. We also had to go to parenting classes. We had our third child. The Division of Social Services was still involved off and on during the next 14 years. My oldest son was the victim of the most physical and emotional abuse, and my husband and I had the courts do a care and protection order to have my son leave home. He was placed with relatives, group homes, and foster homes. This was very difficult for him, and he started acting out with all kinds of bad behaviors. His acting out with emotional and physical behavior was because the other siblings got to stay home with their parents and he was not allowed to. Two continued to be emotionally abused.

My husband filed for divorce. That year, I went to my first psychiatric hospitalization for depression, post-traumatic stress disorder, and bipolar disorder; I was there for five days. I was asked not to be with the children without supervision. Due to my psychiatric issues, I was acting out on the kids. I was asked me to leave my home. I started out in a homeless shelter, and from there I lived out of a tent at a campground. Everything started to go downhill. I was being hospitalized every month, and sometimes it was for being suicidal. I hated my life, and this is where I blamed my father for what he did to me. I focused so intensely on the abuse I received as a child and blamed my situation on my father and what he did to me. I was approved for affordable housing, and I moved. The building was for seniors and those with disabilities.

I used food as a comfort. I tried a day group treatment program, which helped with some of my issues, but I never really got rid of my anger at the world. I started receiving Electronic Convulsive Treatments (ECT), which were shocks to my brain cells. This was supposed to help with the depression, but it never made a difference. It made things worse. I received so many shock treatments within a ten-year period that it caused severe memory loss. My memory is still horrible. I got married when I wasn't ready and had three children who were mistreated. My mom had moved and wasn't able to support me in the same way from afar. My older brother was trying to help me with the medical issues, and my younger sister was standing by me and helped me with the emotional aspects.

While in the mental health system I was qualified for a Rehab program. They would help me get a job or send me to college. I went to college to become a teacher in a daycare setting. I went to school, and I did not finish. The courses I took were at night, and I only took two at a time. At that time, I was harming myself and was in and out of psychiatric hospitals. I used alcohol with my meds, I tried to overdose, and I even cut my wrist. I hated the world and myself and was very quiet and withdrawn. I only did what I had to. I went to a day program, which was made up of different groups recovering from mental health issues.

I was coming home from an ECT, and I met another tenant. I don't remember how she introduced herself to me, but it has been a very long and solid friendship. She is much older than me, and it feels like she's a mother to me. We have been through a lot together; I feel I owe her so much. She would check on me when I went into isolation, and she was always there for me to talk to. She has helped me get out of my closed-door apartment and helped keep me from being so withdrawn. Now, I try to help her out as much as I can with her medical issues. I feel like I owe it to her.

My issues played a huge role in my life. I started gaining weight and not eating well. I reached my all-time highest weight of 300 lbs. Around that time my friend shared with me about her weight loss surgery and how it might help me. I decided I wanted to try weight loss surgery. I went to a weight loss clinic. The doctors there said I couldn't have the surgery because I had been in a psychiatric hospital within the past two years. The reason for this, they told me, if I remember correctly, was they don't know if I would be able to follow the guidelines for postoperative care. They still allowed me to see them, and they watched my weight, and it was up and down, but mostly I was gaining. I was upset with them for not doing the surgery, and I didn't take the program seriously. So, I left the clinic.

I attended the new weight loss clinic, and they gave me a different response to having the weight loss surgery. I was approved. I went through the preoperative process, but it took me a while. I needed to lose 15% of my weight before they could do the surgery. During this process, I was learning to be more aware of the foods I was eating, but I continued to sabotage myself with the food in other ways. I had the gastric bypass surgery 4 years ago. Things went well for me, and I followed the liquid meals phase. After the surgery, the nutritionist saw the patients. I lied about what I was eating. The transitioning to regular foods was difficult. I was playing around, not taking the idea that I might have an addiction, seriously. I thought it was a joke, and I certainly did not believe it. I began to gain weight. This weight gain went on for quite a while, and I gained back about forty pounds.

Two years ago, I started going to the self-help group. I didn't take it seriously. After the meetings, I would be really upset, and my friend and I would go out to eat. I was feeling that the group leader was trying to make me see I could be a food addict. After one of the meetings, I decided not to return to the group. I felt ganged up on and thought that I didn't need this turmoil in my life. When I went to see the nutritionist once a week, I vented my anger about what the group leader was saying about food addiction. I refused to go for quite a while. When I did go back and try again, it started to hit me: maybe I am a food addict. I kept going, and changes were happening. My eating was improving, and I began to share in therapy. Then the big day came when I admitted I had a food addiction. This was a huge step for me to admit in front of people. I started reading the literature, carrying it in my bags always. I talked to people about staying away from my triggers, and I was fully on board with recovery, and I continue to live this way.

I have a plan of eating, and I can follow it. I have been abstinent for two years now, no sugar, flour, or wheat. I do _A online meetings and other meetings online. I have lost over 125 lbs. I am in the process of looking for a sponsor and started attending a weekly face-to-face meeting. I see I have been making headway in my life. I want to thank the weight loss clinic, my psychologists, my therapists, and my friends, who are helping me deal better with my issues. Working with other food addicts has been the most helpful treatment for this disease. If I didn't have the groups, I would be listening to the naysayers in my life, drowning myself in food and self-pity. I feel like a new person. For the first time in my life, I can say I am actively trying not to enable others and people please all of the time. I have found that by not enabling others, I am giving them much more room to grow and take care of themselves. This alone has made a big difference because I am learning to take care of myself.

Since I admitted I was a food addict and stopped eating sugar, flour, and wheat I have found I can make strides to being and feeling healthy both with my physical and mental illness. Before I admitted I was a food addict, I felt like I was climbing a mountain with the weight of the world on my shoulders. I had to travel so far and walk through so much pain to know what it feels like to be loved. So many people have been showing me love and giving me love for so many years, and today I am so grateful to be able to receive that for myself. I deserve it! I have found what love is and now I am trying to reach out to people I left behind. I do still have issues that come, and some main ones are people pleasing and not telling people what I'm feeling or when they have hurt me. I do feel great sharing this with you, and I hope that you, the reader, might be able to take some of this in and know that you're not the only one out there. There is support for you too, and I hope you're able to reach out and take it in.

A song helped me through all my pain, and even with the pain, and I came out the other side.

"I gotta take a little a little time, A little time to think things over what love is.

H.'S STORY

I remember I got hooked on carbs and sugars at a very early age. My parents were divorced. My sister and I lived with my mother, and my father used to visit us once or twice a month. He used to bring us a lot of foods I don't eat now, and I remember I regularly went to the place we stored them to have another pack of something. Since that early age, at about 7, the only thing that made sense for me, the only thing that kept me attentive, interested, and excited, was food. I remember I couldn't get calm if I didn't eat everything my father had brought. It was a similar story with my sister, but not really. My mom was powerless and kept begging us to allocate the foods my father had brought for all the upcoming days of the month. We couldn't because we wanted to try everything. We didn't get much of these foods during the days he was gone. However, I was different than my sister. There wasn't fancy food around, most of the time, but that was not the cause of my overeating. I overate during 'normal' days, too, with whatever food we had in the house. I was a hopeless compulsive eater and food addict. I couldn't focus on anything else than food. I was absent-minded, depressed, and unhappy at the times between eating, and I used carbs and sugars to lift me up.

I gained weight at the age of 9. I was always one of the biggest kids in school and later, one of the biggest people at the University. Although I don't come from big numbers, I always felt unhappy about my weight. I also got pain in my leg due to the weight I had. I remember dieting unsuccessfully for almost all my adolescent life. I would starve myself and exercise, buying into the lie that after a certain amount of time spent on a diet, I would be able to eat carbohydrates and sugars normally. This was my obsession – to eat these and not gain weight. I couldn't though. I always ended up having more than I had told myself I would have. I can never have one bite of these with impunity. I always end up in a terrible binge. My food addiction took over. I stole my friends' food, my in-law's food, and my employers' food. I stole, cheated, lied, and hid to get my addiction satisfied. The more I did it, the less it satisfied.

Thankfully, I found a 12-step program that gives me freedom from the hell of eating grains, carbs, and sugars. Moreover, it gives me peace of mind. As my disease progressed unaddressed into anorexia and bulimia, I realized I couldn't heal it by myself. I needed help from someone who had suffered like me and had found a solution. I tried, and I failed on a regular basis until I got desperate. I then was ready to submit to any suggestions provided in the 12-step program I am part of. I commit my food to another person. At first, I tried to eat what they told me to eat but without commitment. It didn't work; it didn't work many times. I ended up bingeing because I believed the lie of "one bite." This bite wasn't necessarily made of sugar or carbs. But I am a compulsive overeater as well; thus, I always ended up unable to control my weight.

Now I am so grateful to have found the solution for me. I eat three abundant, healthy, delicious meals a day; I am a part of a growing community filled with decent people who want to make a difference for themselves and the world; and I have peace of mind at the times between my meals. This is nothing short of a miracle for a person who at every waking hour was always busy with trying to control what to eat, how much, and when to get slim.

What a strange word! For some, this means something to do with sex! In this context, it is abstinence from substances over which I have no control or over which I believe I need control. If I need to control, I probably don't have the control. So, abstinence is the only solution. With that abstinence comes freedom. I no longer have the phenomenon of craving that is a particular substance calling for its friends once it is inside my body. I have choices. I have the space between the impulse and the action. I am free in a way I have never known before. You too can have this freedom.

Isolation

On the Myers–Briggs, my score on the introvert/extrovert measure lies very close to the center. Thus, I am rarely content, as I am pressing my introverted self to be more into extroverted or conversely my extroverted self to be more introverted. No one is happy. To find the balance for me and perhaps many others is to find a place in which I spend time with others conversing, laughing, experiencing life. However, I must find a place in time in which I pray, meditate, breathe, walk and think my own thoughts while humming my own tunes. I strive to stay out of isolation and in relationship, not only with others but more importantly with myself and the universe.

Sadomasochism

I have engaged in this set of behaviors; however, for those who have not apparently done so, one might be surprised to see the unmanageability of hurting oneself or another or allowing others to hurt me or my family or friends. These hurts might be physical, emotional, traumatic, in times of war, or unintentional. Sometimes, when gravel abrades the skin with a fall from a bicycle, the pain of cleaning the wound may be greater than the initial injury; however, cleansing is necessary. So many of my food-related behaviors and emotional triggers are connected to reliving the harms of the past. When I can cleanse these injuries, the wounds can finally heal from the inside out. I no longer need the food to soothe me. Therapy can help but ABSTINENCE provides the milieu in which I do the work of therapy and support groups to change my relationship with trigger foods and behavior. This takes time.

Sunshine

At one time in my life, I flew in and out of a major international airport. It was not uncommon for the coastal fog to surround the plane for a few minutes on the ground and then we took off through the clouds into the sunshine. That experience became a metaphor for my life awareness that the sunshine is often close at hand. I may need to fly to see it. Except at night the sun is almost always shining above the clouds. Note to self: if you don't change what you are doing today, your tomorrows will look like yesterday or previews of past attractions.

Food Coma

Most of us have experienced this phenomenon on Thanksgiving or other holidays in which we have over imbibed or overeaten. It can be the 3PM slump. It can be the naptime in the mid-morning or the after-dinner snooze. For me, it was connected to substances to which I was allergic. When I stopped eating these things, my energy dramatically stabilized.

Hormones

This might be a whole book by itself. The short version is that I was molested as a seven-year-old and suffered hormonal changes for the rest of my life. I often experienced testosterone driven desires and emotions more akin to those of my male friends than my female friends. I had monthly menstrual cycles that ended in 24 hours of pain similar to birthing but with no offspring. During my menstrual cycling years, I learned that under the effects of one ovary I was often suicidal and under the effects of the opposite ovary I was often homicidal. I did not realize this for many years because of the two-month cycle. Perimenopause and menopause were challenging but reliefs. Even years after my last menses I found that I had cycles that were 31 days apart. Emotional tumult still accompanied what would've been the beginning of my period, had I still had menses. Without the visual component, this too took me years to realize.

I had completed a master's degree thesis on PMS or as it was called then premenstrual syndrome. Later, the sort of experience I described was called late luteal phase dysphoric disorder (LLPDD). One of the interviewees was a man whose wife had PMS/LLPDD, and he suggested that the best thing t he could do to help his wife was to keep track of her menses. When she was becoming distressed emotionally or physically, he and his calendar "knew" why. Just that information often resolved upsets before they became conflagrations.

Calendaring emotions (t for tears, T for TEARS, u for upset, U for UPSETS, a for anger, R for rage, etc.) might serve to document the transitions easily.

Additional documentation is easily acquired using a basal thermometer before arising and charting the temperatures. My documentation showed me that seven days from the beginning of my menses, I experienced a change in temperature and often a day of consternation. 14 days from the onset of my menses I noted other temperature changes, and in my case, the drop in progesterone from then through the beginning of my next menses marked emotional distress and the LLPDD above. The onset of my menses while a relief from the emotional pain of the preceding two weeks, brought with it the excruciating physical pain of cramps, vomiting, diarrhea, and the loosening of my pelvis with the tightening of the muscles between knee and hip.

One doctor hearing the description of the above from my mother said, "Now, now, Mrs.," as though he knew what birth pains were. I doubt that did. Another doctor who saw me in the condition described above told me that he would get some morphine for me. He returned unable to obtain the morphine but held my hand while the Demerol he gave me warmed me up from the feet and head to meet in the middle.

One of the milder hormonal changes was the experience of placemaking that occurred within the 24 hours before my menses starting. I felt an incredible urge to clean, tidy up, prepare with readiness for what was to come. I have heard this to be true in the hours before birthing also. There are many times after my menses ceased, I wished I had had this monthly experience of desire for cleanliness and tidying.

Brainstorming/heart storming

For years in my teaching career, I taught creative problem-solving, aka Paul Torrance. The practice of brainstorming solutions to problems or challenges became an ingrained part of me. Allowing ideas to come willy-nilly without judgment or limitation presented possibilities. The heart storming aspect of this is allowing the heart freedom in the same way that the brainstorming dealt with offering solutions there, that are compassionate, empathetic, tolerant, and kind. It's amazing when one heart storms and brainstorms to identify potential solutions.

SoyNut Butter Cookies

An example of a solution is that one day I was longing for peanut butter cookies. I wanted them to be moist and peanut-buttery with those little crosshatches on top and fresh from the oven in time for lunch. Recipe time: I took 1 ounce of wheat germ, one egg, 1 ounce of soy nut butter, half an ounce of butter with cinnamon, nutmeg, vanilla flavoring and mixed thoroughly. I took teaspoons full and placed them on the sprayed cookie sheet, smoothed the edges, and cross-hatched the tops with my fork. Baked at 350° until cooked, I was taking them from the oven when a friend came into the house. She was surprised at my cookies. She asked, "And how many of those can you have?" I responded that I could have all of them! I didn't tell her that, in addition, I was taking 2 ounces of Greek yogurt mixed with cinnamon and sweetener to make the frosting! (There were a lot of cookies. I was quite sated by the time I finished eating them all.) Sweeteners and flavors are optional. I used them then.

Portable Puffin

Most of us don't want to be too puffed up about ourselves as this indicates a lack of humility; however, to have them often named after one may not be as laudable as some things. With this muffin, the name changes with each iteration. Please take it as your own and pass it on.

> 1 ounce of wheat germ
> one egg
> two ounces of salsa
> 1 ounce of gjetost cheese cut into tiny pieces
> a pinch of baking soda
> an ounce of sesame seeds or caraway seeds
> half an ounce of butter or oil
> mix thoroughly in a coffee mug, and microwave for three minutes. Pop into a plastic bag. Add three whole raw vegetables and voila: lunch is served.

Migraines

The bane of my existence for 40 years were sporadic migraines sending me off to bed in a darkened room with the half of my head screaming for relief. My eyes were closed against the piercing light, sometimes with blocks of opalescent light stacked circularly to interrupt my vision, along with intermittent vomiting and diarrhea, and pain in my nasal passages that demanded my teeth be extracted. All this came as a result of barometric pressure changes, smog in the Los Angeles basin, and some mixture of tension and stress interwoven in the formula.

I had experienced the earliest migraines when I went to college at UC Santa Barbara. When the wind blew the eucalyptus trees' leaves between the campus and Isla Vista, I knew I had a short time before I would need to be in bed.

Years later, having had many interruptions of work and play due to migraines, I went to the major hospital to their experts at the headache and pain clinic. Daily doses of 400 mg of B2 and 200 mg of CoQ10 were recommended to me. These helped but did not remove the migraines. A friend of mine was going to see a famous doctor. She suggested I meet her there. I didn't think it sounded like fun, but I went. After psychological and brain tests, he suggested GABA and inositol might alleviate my distress caused by what he said were brain misfires. Adding Brain Calm or Brain Calm Plus. To my daily regime removed the migraines. My life opened.

(Please check with your medical professionals before trying what worked for me. There can be contraindications).

Passionate Pursuits

There've been two kinds of passionate pursuits in my life: one destructive and the other productive. The former probably was the result of hormonal changes that came as a result of being molested as a child and of taking into my body the uncontained guilt and shame of the perpetrator. I lived with a body that had entirely too much testosterone for a female gendered person. My rages and my sexual passion were more akin to those of males in my life than to those of females.

The second productive set of passionate pursuits have included making pottery on a wheel under a famous potter, as he was student of a teacher of Bauhaus fame; genealogy; photography; teaching Romeo and Juliet; studying with a professor from behind the Iron Curtain from Prague about the language of poison in heart and body and mind; writing poetry; swimming in waters filled with iridescent sea life and splashing moonbeams; striving to aid others toward surrender and consistency and victory in their battles with addictions; the provision of appropriately challenging education to gifted children; the support to become a reader and speaker of standard English; and as a guest to add to the health professionals' interview: "Do you struggle with limiting your consumption of sugar or other foods?" I continue to delight and to acknowledge, food addiction is real and treatment is abstinence from trigger foods and behaviors in passionate pursuits of the productive variety daily.

Quality of Life

Many times, I have thought about the quality of life I would like to experience. Sometimes in my thoughts, the quantity of money that I had was the focus of attention. Other times I focused on relationships. Today my focus on the quality of life has more to do with the absence of addictions and the quality of relationships that come as a result. Healing and maturing are two aspects prerequisite to the quality of life I now desire. In a chiropractic pamphlet, the description of the root of many health problems was given as imbalance. I believe that to be true in terms of the body, mind, emotion, and spirit.

Alignment in the physical body with better posture awareness of the foot as having four corners on which there are imaginary tires and my job is to keep all four tires on the road. Alignment in the mind, for me, encourages active learning and lifelong learning, alignment of emotions encourages mindfulness, meditation, and allowing the recovery from resentments, grudges, and upsets of the heart. Spiritual alignment means to me today alignment with the universe, and its timing and the movement toward good or some people call it GOD or good orderly direction. To achieve these daily and over time require support, integration, and balance. The movement away from chaos or rigidity toward a central flow is another way to think of this integrative process.

Freedom from Pain

At those times I have struggled with excruciating pain, the freedom from pain seemed the largest that I could give myself. Migraines, sciatic pain, lower back pain, headaches, gastroesophageal problems, metatarsal problems, inguinal nerve problems, impinged nerve problems, muscle and nerve pain resulting from car accidents and sports injuries, arthritis, infections, the delayed total hip replacement, even hangnails have created physical pain that distressed my entire system. Relief from these came through vitamins, massage, trigger point massage, aromatherapy, medicines, orthotics, surgery, injections, heat and cold packs, antibiotics, and band-aids well mixed with time. I have been responsible for going to the doctor or other health practitioners to attain knowledgeable advice, to practice what was offered to me, and to return to achieve better results until they became optimal results. When the pain has been emotional pain, there have been other alternatives: a specialist to assess and address particulars.

To address pain by remediating the causes I have used Pilates, 1:1 Gyrokinesis, restorative yoga, bubble baths, showers, transcendental meditation, mindfulness practices ala Dr. Dan Siegel (Mindfulness Co Director at UCLA Mindfulness Clinic) and Jon Kabat-Zinn Mindfulness-based relaxation system at UMass, massages, naps, reading science fiction or fantasy books in a series, praying, yelling at God, movies on TV or in a theater, isolation tank, no grain, no sugar, no alcohol, no lemon juice, not eating tyramine (not eating meats or vegetables left in the refrigerator more than three days), taking a combination of B2 and co-Q10 and GABA and inositol and B complex and D3 and C and Omegas, drinking water, sleeping about eight hours in each 24, taking photos (to focus outside of my body), taking walks that got longer, painting, doing genealogy, doing monochromes, taking a class, participating with the doctor and nurse and psychologist in a chronic pain group (I was not alone and others with diabetes, missing limbs, and other causes for the experience of chronic pain). "This too shall pass" as a mantra with "thy will not mine be done", breathing, counting breaths in healing and breath out as pain, chanting Om nava chivaya gurave, the Anusara yoga invocation, listening to music, smelling lavender, NSAID nonsteroidal anti-inflammatory prescription pads cut to place on painful areas, over-the-counter pain relievers, acupuncture, acupressure, abstaining from nightshade vegetables, use of an amazing piece of equipment which wrapped the surgical area and was filled with ice water and whenever the pain increased I was to drain the device and add for a new ice water, frozen peas in a bag applied to the hurting area externally, elevating or supporting with pillows, cortisone shots, hypnosis, an expert in myofascial pressure points, a shaman, a friend who kept saying, "there is a solution", a nerve block for shoulder surgery, masturbation to focus and then relieve tension, sexual activity with a loving partner, non-sexual activity with a loving partner, gratitude lists, thankfulness, talking with the therapist, doctor or friend, tens machine, physical therapy, chiropractic therapy, contra, energy work gentle touch, exercise and tenacity. Perseverance. If these don't work for you, you will identify your own.

Sometimes just the certainty that I know my body is not right plus persistent tenacity to find a better solution has helped me find a doctor who could identify the problem and an appropriate solution. Once I felt that I wanted to die: I was in such abominable abdominal pain. After many tests and suggestions that my problem was mental and my continued plea for a physical solution to a physical problem, a barium upper GI test identified the beginnings of a small ulcer in my transverse colon. Prescription for an appropriate antacid medicine and some changes in diet transformed my life with the cessation of pain. Perseverance in taking the next indicated action with a prayer for guidance to the next indicated action **and next** to make possible what some people call miracles.

Dancing to music is exercise which exorcises the demons: automatic negative thoughts! Walking 10,000 (to 20,000 steps each day helps enjoying days past 60 years of age due to slower metabolism: my current goal up to consideration!) I'm still doing genealogy and photography and traveling with my beloved.

BARRY ELDER (PSEUDONYM); A STORY ABOUT POWERLESSNESS OVER FOOD

It was not until 1986 when I was 46 years old that I had even the smallest inkling that I was addicted to specific food substances. I look back now with thirty years of abstinence from my binge foods - added-sugar, wheat, excess fat, salt, artificial sweeteners, caffeine, alcohol and, possibly, large volumes of any food; I haven't binged out of control. I lost over 80 pounds of excess weight and stayed at 179 plus/minus three pounds, and I have slowly acquired an emotional and spiritual peace which, when I began food addiction recovery, was simply unimaginable.

Part One

It now looks to me that my food addiction began in the womb, or before, through the passing of genetic material which made me predisposed to chemical dependency. Maude, my chronically obese grandmother, died at age 52 of a massive heart attack while struggling to stay perfectly on a rice and orange juice diet, the latest prescription of her doctor; she loved her sweets (including sugar in the juice) and her grains (like the rice). My lovable kindergarten teacher grandma was probably a late stage food addict. Her lawyer and school principal husband died at 42 from complete liver failure. If you put that medical information together with his habit of going off for days to drink with his railroad worker buddies, we would now say the underlying cause of death was advanced alcoholism.

As early as I can remember, my favorite foods were ice cream, candy, toast with butter and cinnamon sugar, and saltines with jelly. This could be attributed to a normal child's sweet tooth, except that I would also get up on a chair as a young child, sneak the syrup off the top shelf, and swig it straight from the bottle. I also stole and ate the top layer of homemade Christmas cookies from dozens of tins set out as presents for relatives and friends. As I grew old enough to go to the corner store by myself (against explicit direction from my parents not to), I started stealing change left out on the dresser after my father went to sleep. I would buy root beer, fudge cycles, cups with chocolate sauce, cupcakes, and a small package of banana bread with thick vanilla icing. Sometimes I thought that "all kids do this," and other times I felt very guilty because I knew that it was all wrong: stealing the money, going out of the house alone, and eating so many sweets. I never got caught, and I never told. Now I see it as early-stage food addiction.

I never wanted to be a thief or to be someone who disobeyed his parents. I wanted the sweet foods – a lot, but I felt disgusted with myself when I ate too much, sometimes to the point that my belly hurt. I didn't like being obsessed with how I would sneak what I wanted, felt guilt, and about the lies I would tell if anyone got in my way. Recently I heard a Pepsi executive trying to minimize sugar addiction by saying, "No one ever robbed a bank to get some ice cream." As a child, the only bank I knew was my father's pile of change and later the bills in his wallet. Getting my "sweet tooth" satisfied led me to steal as much as I thought I could without getting caught. This was the beginning of my being powerless over specific foods.

There is one memory that I have slowly recovered in abstinence, which I now see as a marker for when I crossed over the line from being a food abuser to being a food addict. I was about six or seven years old, and it was the holiday season. After coming home from school, I went to the kitchen and opened the refrigerator. I just liked to look. To my surprise, there were two very large roles of sugar cookie dough. I couldn't take my eyes off them. I had long ago developed a taste for raw sugar cookie dough. Mom was preparing to bake and make gift tins, but as I looked an idea crossed my mind. "If I untapped one of the rolls and cut a very thin slice off the end, then no one would know." I had not opened the fridge thinking I would actually eat anything. I just liked to look. However, now there was a debate going on in my mind. "Do I really want to go through all the trouble just for a thin slice of raw dough?" "Is it really true that I would not be caught?" "What if I did?" "If someone asks me about it, isn't it a sin to tell a lie?" Several times, I almost closed the refrigerator door and went out to play. Then, the pull of the food.... Finally, I took one of the rolls out and unwrapped it. I was just going to check it out to see if deception was possible, but it was as if I was in a trance. I cut a sliver, ate it, loved it, and decided that just one more sliver would not be noticed. I was feeling excited and kept cutting and eating without stopping until several inches of cookie dough was "gone." "Uh-oh..."

I had gone too far. I felt scared, guilty, ashamed and angry at myself. I had the thought, "Well, if I might get caught anyway, I might as well keep eating," and that is what I did. I had the thought, "If I eat the whole roll then maybe no one will notice it is gone." It was a crazy idea, even crazier that at times it seemed to make sense. At first, there were hits from the sweet taste each time I cut another piece. Then I started having a sort of rancid feeling in my mouth as if it was too sweet. I kept eating. It didn't even occur to me that it would be better to stop. I didn't think of it this way at the time, but I was eating out of control like when I started eating Oreo cookies or chocolate covered graham crackers out of the bag. I was so focused on eating more and in almost a frenzy I doubt I could have stopped even if I wanted to, but it didn't even occur to me to do so.

I remember when I had eaten over half of the roll. I was getting a little groggy, and my stomach was beginning to hurt. Now I did consider stopping, but I couldn't. I just kept eating. In the end, I was actually miserable. I estimated that I had put over two pounds of raw dough in my little stomach. I ached. I felt something akin to nauseous. I did not stop. After the whole roll was gone I remember actually thinking about taking out the other one and continuing to eat. It seemed crazy, but that is what I seemed to want to do. The only thing that stopped me was that I knew it would be impossible. I went back to my room, got busy with an incomplete project drawing my toys. I was hurting, very uncomfortable from the binge. I tried to focus on drawing to take my mind off the pain. Sometimes it worked. Most of the time it did not. Suddenly my mother came into my room. "Honey, do you know what happened to the second roll of sugar cookie dough?" Busted! I pretended I did hear her question, didn't even notice she was in the room. She was persistent, asking me again and again. Finally, I turned around, looked her in the eyes and said as calmly and sincerely as I could, "I didn't even know there was cookie dough in the fridge." I was scared but tried not to show it. I didn't want to be a kid who lied to his mother, but what else could I do. Simply telling the truth and apologizing seemed out of the question.

My mother kept asking - the same question over and over. "I know I made two big rolls. Are you sure you don't know anything about it?" "No, Mom, I really don't," I kept lying, now knowing that I wasn't telling the truth and still trying to act as if I was. At one point I remember my mother's face contort as if she knew she had made a double batch, and she and I were the only ones in the house. She couldn't believe her little boy would lie about something like this. Finally, she just gave up, turned sound and went back to the kitchen. Actually, that is not the end of the memory for me. I remember being very relieved when she gave up - and still scared and still a little guilty and ashamed. But that went away, and I have the vague memory that I started believing that I hadn't done anything wrong, maybe didn't really blood anything - not even eat all that dough.

Our memories play a trick on us, but one thing I am sure about now that didn't even occur to me at the time or for decades afterward: I was definitely powerless in the situation. I was powerless over the first thought to just look in the refrigerator, powerless over how my mind lit up when I saw the new roll of cookie dough, powerless over having the idea of eating just a sliver, and, at one point, powerless over taking another bite and then another. A physical craving beyond my control caused some or all of that. That's not all. More subtly but also devastatingly I was powerless over the lying. As a child, I know that I did not want to be someone who lied to his mother. I certainly did not want to be someone who lied to myself and then started believing the lies. I think that the idea of sneaking some food by slivering didn't feel right, but it overpowered my basic morals against cheating. Certainly, I did not want to lie to my mother, but again I was like an addict protecting his stash. No, not "like," I was an addict protecting my stash, and at the time, my food addict personality completely hijacked the personality of my higher self, the personality of my true heart and soul.

Some will say that I am being too hard on a very young boy. I don't make this point to moralize or put myself down; I was doing that already to myself as a child. Rather, I bring up the issue to simply say that the seed of a severe food addiction was already planted and growing well in me, no blame, at a very early age.

Part Two

There was little dramatic evidence of food addiction during my grade school and high school years. Living at home, my meals were all planned and cooked by my mother. I became very active athletically swimming competitively from age ten, playing football, basketball, and track in junior high and high school. Summers were soon spent at Boy Scouts camp where I was put on staff when I was twelve. The rest of the time, when I wasn't eating, sleeping or in school, I was studying or working on an extra-curricular project. I made top grades by working hard and did the same with my hobbies. I was one of the youngest in a boys program, played piano in a dance band, did several science projects, edited the high school literary magazine, and wrote a weekly youth column for the town newspaper. I didn't have much time or opportunity to overeat.

A lot was hidden. Unlike young women who are valued for their slim figures, I as a young man was valued for how much I could eat, how big I was and how fast I would eat. "He eats like a man." "No one will push him around." "Look how fast he chows down and then gets to his studies or out to practice." I always had heaping servings and usually had seconds. I'd come home and put all the pieces in a loaf of Wonder Bread out on the table, add a lot of butter and sugar, and eat it all without stopping. Sometimes this felt a little off, but I wasn't gaining weight, and most of the time I was encouraged for having a healthy appetite.

There were exceptions. Once, my parents asked me to slow down while I was eating dinner with them. I tried as hard as I could, but I couldn't. I actually finished just after they had started. That was embarrassing.

Often in church, all I could think about were pretty girls and going out to eat afterward where I would always binge on a four-inch-high sandwich, double order of French Fries, large soda and an special desert with six scoops of different ice creams and several toppings. I went into a zone thinking about nothing but eating. As I look back, the adrenaline of competitive academics, sports, and endless projects replaced the worst highs of addictive eating. When I went away to college, all that changed. My mother no longer controlled my food, and there were free unlimited seconds at the cafeteria. I not only took complete advantage but also, when the food line closed, I waited out my peers, so I could finish what they left on their plates. I started going out at night for "snacks." I played football and couldn't play sports. My weight started edging up.

I started trying to control my weight. Late in my freshman year, I started wearing trench coat ALL the time, in my classes and my room. I postured "cool" but the real message, which I actually believed, was that "if you can't see my growing belly, then I'm not really getting fat." About the same time, I started skipping breakfast. I told myself that this was so I could start studying earlier. The truth? It was my first diet and the beginning of anorexia. By sophomore year I was often not eating breakfast or lunch. During junior year I was not eating any meals (but going out and bingeing late). All this while I was still overeating whenever I did go to the college mess more than one day at a time AND before I graduated "fasting."

In my senior year, I had what we all called a "nervous breakdown." I had returned home for three months for psychiatric help. The precipitating event was my girlfriend leaving me for another man. As I look back, I now think of this as my first adult "bottom" as an addict. I certainly lost control of my relationship, but also, I was now restricting two or three days at a time, still gaining weight, and my school work was also spinning out of control. All of this shattered my illusion of control, confronting me with the deep self-centered fear that is at the core of food addiction and every other addiction.

Part Three

After college, my food addiction really began to show. I now think of this period as my Dieting Years. I kept gaining weight, and I assumed that I could take care of the problem like I believed everyone else did – by going on a diet. It was all about "calories in and calories out." My first diet was merely trying to eat less. I did this for a couple of months with no problem, and I lost weight. I went back to eating "normally," and I started gaining again. My second effort at dieting was counting calories. This worked, too. As long as I counted every day, I kept losing. However, when I figured I had lost enough weight and stopped counting, I soon was bursting out of my pants.

At one point I realized I had to look at this problem more seriously. I read "Nutrition in a Nutshell" and all the healthy eating books by Adel Davis. I started logging everything that I put into my mouth, slowly developing my own personal guidelines. I made my own complex and carefully measured familiar for breakfast along with a pre-prepared yeast drink. For lunch, I made myself huge salads, and for dinner, I began some serious cooking. I cooked my own honey whole wheat bread, steamed brown rice with different spices, and stir-fried vegetables with all possible proteins in a wok. I ate a piece of fruit or a fruit smoothie for dessert. Soon my weight was back on track. I kept up the planning and recording of my meals for more than a year. At that point, I added in another goal: trying to demonstrate that this healthy eating could be done inexpensively. I learned to cook 25 cent meals and shared this with others. I was adding a "lifestyle change" to my dieting.

One day I realized that I was bursting out of my clothes. I had gained over twenty-five pounds, and I had no idea how it had happened. Well, I had stopped recording my food, thinking "I don't have to do this anymore," and "I can indulge myself every once in a while." Sometimes the indulgence was sweets. Other times it was just an extra serving or two the main course. I went back to not eating breakfast, also sometimes skipping lunch. I didn't lose weight, but I did stop gaining. I found a special diet. Almost immediately, I started bingeing on protein – lamb, chicken, pork, occasionally fish, but mostly beef steak. I started feeling like I was on speed, that seemed to give me the energy to do more. The more I binged on steak and kept away from the carbs, the more weight I lost. I started alternating between Stillman to lose and intermittent partial fasting to maintain. I didn't like being "on speed" all the time. After a few months, I stopped doing both. I packed back on the fat.

If my clothes didn't fit, I'd go back on. I'd focus on different proteins. Once I ate mostly lamb, another time mostly pork. I'd slip back to normal eating, and my weight would sneak up again. I noticed the pattern but didn't make anything of it. Sequential dieting was my coping mechanism, and I thought I had it under control. I went on to try other diets for variety – the beer and wine diet, vegetarianism, a pre-diabetic exchange diet, macrobiotics, the powder diet, drinking a lot of water all day. They all worked. There was one new development; my top weight and my lower weight kept going up. I would diet and lose weight, then, as I began saying, "something happened." I started feeling anxious and frustrated more of the time, especially when I was almost 50 pounds over my "feel good" weight. I never once considered that I might be in some way powerless. All I could see was that I could regularly lose weight and all I had to do was lose weight better, as I said to myself "learn to do maintenance" – keep it off. I tried to figure this out but couldn't come up with a solution to the problem.

During my Dieting Years, I was always dieting. At least, one new effort a year. The cycle was: diet/lose weight/"something happened"/gain weight back/repeat. It wasn't until much later, about ten years into food addiction abstinence and recovery, that I recovered the memories regarding what "something happened" really was. It was very simple: when I felt that I had reached the weight goal on my diet, I rewarded myself, and how did I reward myself? By going out to a restaurant and "eating my head off," or by eating a half gallon of chocolate ice cream or buying coffee cake and eating it all, or by eating a whole bag of cookies – sometimes all of the above.

Basically, I was always dieting or gaining weight. "Something happened" was a binge or series of binges on foods to which I later discovered I was becoming progressively chemical dependent. At the time of the bingeing, it never occurred to me that there was anything abnormal about going into binge mode after a diet. "I deserve a reward." "Isn't that what everyone does?" Of course, I didn't check it out. It didn't occur to me to do that either. Without even the thought that there may be something off about my "rewards," I was powerless to do anything different. Moreover, information about "something happened" didn't come up in my memory when I tried to figure it out. I just didn't exactly remember what had happened. After all, I was able to stop bingeing. It was all a subtle but powerful pattern of euphoric recall that took over my conscious mind.

I could always remember quite vividly my major "treat" foods and how good they made me feel, but I had no memory of the consequences. Like how I would do most of my binges in private, how I always ate more than I had intended to eat, how I ate passed feeling uncomfortably full, and how I would always feel guilty and depressed. The solution to any of these problems that came to mind was frequently "eat more" or "eat again soon." In light of my later recovery this was insane reasoning, but at the time I was powerless. It simply seemed completely reasonable in the moment and then I could not remember it as significant at all later when I tried to analyze my own problem. My mind only remembered the highs and forgot the lows. That was powerlessness.

Towards the end of this period, I began stealing food and eating it while I shopped. At first, it was just eating cashews or candy out of the open bins. Then I started picking up a large bag of my favorite cookies e.g. several kinds of chocolate – and eating them casually as I shopped. One time I put the empty bag on the counter and paid for it at check out, but this made me feel very embarrassed, so I stopped doing that. Instead, I hid the empty bag on a shelf on the sly.

Towards the end, I started wearing clothes that let me stuff a lot of junk food in the pockets. The best was a big army jacket. I went back and forth down the candy aisle, the cookie aisle, and the bakery section stealing all I could stuff in the jacket while picking up my "normal" groceries and putting them in the cart. I had plenty of money to buy all the food I wanted, including the junk food, but I stole it, taking more and more risks at getting caught. For several years, I was as obsessed with stealing in the grocery store as I was with bingeing on it afterward. One time in a city where I was a leader in some innovative work that would have been ruined if I got caught stealing and reported to the press, I could not stop stuffing candy in my army jacket or keep from eating it compulsively as soon as I got out of the store. I was aware of the danger as I did it, and I hardly even considered stopping.

At the end of this period, I went to the doctor for a general check-up. He said that my blood pressure and cholesterol readings were dangerously high. If I didn't lose a lot of weight and keep it off, I was likely to have a heart attack within ten years. What was my response? I thought that I probably couldn't lose weight and keep it off, so I decided to stop going to the doctor. Now that was crazy too. Rather than tell the doctor I couldn't do what he was suggesting and ask for help, I decided his advice was useless and ruled him out of my life. That seemed reasonable to me! Regarding my eating and weight, I had lost the ability to tell the sane from the insane, and I was not even aware of being so out of control. That was really powerlessness.

Part Four

When I began seeing my problem as "not being able to maintain my weight loss after dieting," this led me to my Therapy Years. If "something happened," what was it? If I was somehow depressed, what were the underlying issues? At the minimum, I needed figure out how to "do maintenance." I never once considered that I might be becoming progressively powerless over physical cravings for specific foods. The thought that I had a real addictive disease, much less somehow be a "food addict," was not even a momentary consideration. I was teaching the history of psychology and theories of counseling in a graduate school at the time, so I began by journaling and trying to psychoanalyze myself. I re-read Freud, Jung, Adler, and Reich. With each theorist, I journaled and discovered new insights which were intellectually stimulating and improved my self-esteem. I could see problems in my childhood which made my sometimes desperate compulsiveness make sense, possibly even a disturbed sexuality which could have caused my "oral" cravings.

From resisting Jung and current disciples, I came upon the idea of "spiritual hunger" which I could be confusing with physical hunger. I had been taken to a prominent Adlerian in my youth, and I now came to grips with the uncomfortable fact that I had lied to this gentle psychiatrist - including when he confronted me about my lying. I seriously played with the possibility that I had a deeply depressed sexuality which was manifesting in out of control eating. There was - and still is - some truth in each of these theories and many more. I read and wrote about my eating problem almost every day for over a year, but I kept on being stumped. What could I do that would effectively resolve these inner conflicts.

Finally, my insistence on self-reliance gave way, and I started working with great intensity with a series of counselors. Each used a different approach. First, I tied "brief" therapy with a practitioner of cognitive behavioral therapy. Why? If there was a quick, effective solution, that's what I wanted. I applied myself as I always did. We went through a handbook of exercises, once a week for over a year. Again, I got some great insights and tried many hopeful new behaviors. For example, I found a number of ways my thinking about food was distorted, and I practiced consciously changing my thinking. When I was helped to see that I had come to the belief that I could never get down to and stay at my ideal weight, I started writing "I am becoming 186," twenty times a day in capital letters, then wrote down all the negative thoughts that came up in small lower case. I was amazed at the rich variety of my negative thinking and how the energy went out of the conflicting thoughts as I did this week after week. I also put signs up all over the house, including on the refrigerator, with "186" in big numbers, and started speaking positive affirmations out loud every morning as I looked in the mirror. I lost some weight and kept it off for several months, but I couldn't keep it up. When I let down on my practice, my overeating and weight gain came right back.

I joined a new human potential movement popular in the 70's. I had been very skeptical, but my wife did the program, and I liked the results. So, I sat for fourteen hours a day in a room. Mostly, we experienced the leader working in depth with one person at a time, followed by a series of experiential exercises. I found it engaging and satisfying. I did more large events and then advanced training. My self-esteem seemed to improve, and the group was support for many challenges in my work life. But after a while "something happened" again. I shifted to a counselor at a Weight Loss Center who focused on me identifying the difficult feelings and irrational thinking underlying my out of control eating. She gave me a pre-diabetic food plan, precisely like the one suggested by my doctor several years before, the doctor I had stopped seeing. Like my previous efforts at dieting, I was able to follow the plan at first and lost about fifty pounds. I was still not close to 186, but my counselor had me focus on something else. She gave me the assignment to identify something I enjoyed other than work and do it.

To my great surprise, I couldn't figure out what I enjoyed. Week after week, she gave me the same assignment: keep doing the diet and focus on identifying what I liked. Over and over I came up blank. This was embarrassing and, when I faced that I could not do something so simple and basic, I felt very uncomfortable. In our sessions she had me focus on exactly what I was feeling in the present. As I sat - in her presence - with myself, the feelings began to leak out. I cried, acknowledged fear, and even got angry. It took weeks, but I finally identified something I enjoyed, taking a long hot bath, and did it. This brought up a whole different set of feelings, and in my therapy sessions, I was supported to do this feeling work too. After just a few months of these sessions, my therapist offered a surprising suggestion. Rather than come to her as a counselor, she suggested I join a class she taught on how to be a client. It was much less expensive, and she said that she thought it would be even more effective.

The class was about a special counseling method referred. The class taught about the theory and practice of directly expressing or discharging any feeling that was present with different partners. Then during the week between classes, everyone would pair up for two-hour sessions in which the first one would be the client and then they would reverse. The "counselor" would mainly "be present" and let the other person emote. Sometimes the counselor would suggest a "direction," essentially something the person "clienting" would do or say which would keep the client discharging or deepen the expression of feelings. These directions were identified mainly by noticing what was already starting to work, often saying a positive thought which contradicted a strongly held negative thought. For example, if I were frustrated by not being able to lose weight, I would be given the phrase to say, "I am losing weight," or "I am just the weight I want and need to be." I would focus on expressing the anger or sadness or exasperation that would be intensified. It's hard to explain, but it was easy to demonstrate, and I - and the other class members - caught on very quickly.

As I learned to discharge - and to support others while they were discharging - I also learned the safety guidelines and was given access to those in the community who had been doing this work for years. I had at least one co-counseling session a week (all free) and went to several weekend retreats led by leaders to support longer and deeper sessions (minimal fees plus lodging and meals). My focus shifted from figuring out how to lose weight and maintain the loss to working regularly on my own unresolved feeling. When I was having a productive session, the direction was often: "Are there any earlier and similar unresolved feelings?" The idea was not to try to analyze the feelings but to go right to doing the emotional healing that wasn't or couldn't be done in the past. Thinking would clear up naturally as the old emotional energy moved through and out of me.

This was a period of deep emotional healing. Like much eating disorder therapy, the underlying principle was, "It is not what you are eating but rather what is eating you." I felt better after every session. There was less "eating me," and over several years I could feel steady emotional progress. I started informally teaching, and, as an innovative college teacher, I found ways to help students let go of learning blocks through the use of the principles. These students generally made more progress, not just academically, but also concerning deeper personal development. This added to my own work satisfaction and my basic self-esteem.

Unfortunately, I did not get down to goal weight, and after a while noticed I was putting on pounds again. I kept having periodic binges, and at one point noticed that the binges were actually getting worse. I tried to apply it and "something happened." I slowly fell away from doing as my eating slowly got out of control again. Maybe it was the other way around, i.e. I started overeating and gaining weight as I stopped doing it. However, I heard from others in the network that counseling had not ever enabled them to get over their recurring problems with obesity. I dove more deeply into my work. I took on a second job. I tried the idea of just accepting being fat. This was a high for a while. I permitted myself to eat anything I wanted. I wanted a lot, and I worked on not feeling guilty or ashamed. My weight got up near 300, and I just stopped weighing.

Then one night after an exceptionally demanding week of work, I went out to eat at my favorite restaurant. I had a few drinks first, then hors-d'oeuvres and more than one basket of bread with butter. I read the newspaper and nibbled. This was great! I ordered the largest and most expensive entree (a habit I had been developing to "reward myself") and a bottle of wine. I had gotten used to eating when already full, whatever that meant. I kept reading as I ate thinking "If I eat slowly, I'll enjoy it longer and be able to eat more." When it was time for dessert, I ordered the largest and the "richest" along with after dinner liquor. I walked home in a food haze and a slightly drunken trance. I threw myself on my bed without even taking my clothes off and quickly fell fast asleep.

In the middle of the night, I woke up sweating with a harsh pain in the left side of my chest. I was a little panicked, having trouble breathing and trying to figure out what was going on. It was then that I noticed that I couldn't move one of my arms. It struck me that I was having a heart attack. I thought of calling 911, but before I even tried to do this, I had the thought "What if they keep me the hospital overnight?" I would miss a large important dinner that I had planned my colleagues at work and the outside evaluators from the accrediting agency. I really didn't want to miss that dinner.

So, I decided to "breath through" the possible heart attack. It is something I had heard people did when they had a particularly bad drug trip. It all seemed to make sense. I focused on my breath and the pain. After a while, I fell asleep. I awoke the next morning. The pain was gone. I could move my arm. I was scared but, I thought, "I got through it!" I was greatly relieved. Then, it struck me, "That was crazy!" I had decided not to call a doctor or to go to the emergency room with a heart attack because I thought it was more important to go to a big feast I had planned at work. "That was crazy!" I kept saying to myself. "That was crazy!" And it was! I could have died trying to make sure I didn't miss a big celebratory meal! At that moment I resolved to change my life completely. "I am going to make controlling my food and controlling my work the most important things in my life. I meant it. It never even occurred to me that I would not be able to do it.

Part Five

I now call the next period in my life the Hopeless Years. There were several things that were going on at the same time. I'll describe one at a time. It all had to do with putting my health first, absolutely – meaning "control my food" and "control my work." The first venture was exercise. Everyone had been telling me "diet and exercise" for years. Ever since the concussion playing football (age 17) I had used the direction "no contact sports" to rationalize "no exercise at all." It was suggested that, at a minimum, I just walk on a regular basis. Finally, I began.

I should have known. I was having trouble walking my overweight body upstairs when I had to, stopping to catch my breath. I decided to just walk around the block. I set out at my usual slow pace, but halfway around the block, I was winded. I had to sit down on the curb. I was shocked. But I got up after a while and finished. The next day I made it around the block without stopping. By the end of the week, I was walking around twice and at a slightly faster pace. I decided I would try jogging. Oh, my! Even when I jogged as slowly as I could, I had to stop quite quickly.

This began a few weeks of alternating between running and walking. I would jog as long as I could and then walk. As soon as I regained my breath and energy, I would start running. At one point, I ran – slowly – around the block several times. So, it went. But it wasn't like when I had been an athlete. Yes, I liked being able to make a little progress each month, but now, I was doing this work "so I would lose weight" or "so I wouldn't get fatter." After a few months, it felt like I was actually jogging. Every day, I had to go through "the wall" of not wanting to run or thinking "I can't do this," but I did. And my weight started melting off. I started to know that it would. I decided to train for a half-marathon.

Here's the bottom line: After about a year and a half, I did run and finished a local half-marathon. And I kept running every day even after it for about a year. I get trying to keep making progress: as I met one goal of running longer or faster, I set the bar a little higher. Then, one day, I started having pain in my legs and knees. Rather than check this out with a doctor or even another experienced runner like the running magazines said to be sure to do, I decided to "run through the pain." It didn't take long before I couldn't run at all...... And I started eating more, and I started gaining weight, and my whole motivation for exercising was lost, and, rather than get help to heal my legs or to find more appropriate exercise, I just eliminated exercise from my life completely — like I had stopped going to the doctor. These are the facts, but even more important, I now see, this seems perfectly reasonable to me. There was one sane thought: I asked myself "What are your major strengths?" "How can you apply them to getting control of your food and weight?"

I decided that being a student was my major strength — and being an innovative educator. I had always made high grades in school, was even in a Scholar of the House program in college where I just wrote a book for my senior year. (This was the year I had a "nervous breakdown" but I also completed the manuscript and did graduate.) Now that I was a well known and highly successful innovator and teacher in higher education. I had been a leader of the national student educational reform movement in the Sixties and had been on the teams that created new learner-centers and performance-based liberal arts colleges in the Seventies. I had written about this work in dozens of books, reports, and articles. Now I was the vice president of the first stand-alone college with individually designed AA., BA, and MA degrees. It was the accreditation of these programs which I had coordinated and celebrated at the fancy formal dinner the day after I had had the heart attack.

So, I decided to design an innovative graduate degree program which had underlying goals of helping me learn how to control my food. It was a 66-credit terminal degree in higher education and human service which met all the standards of traditional academic graduate standards, also the standards for learning-center education (each of the courses was self-designed with the approval of a Ph.D. in the field, and also, they were the highest performance-based standards. So, if I was demonstrating counseling skills, I had to show I had met the competencies of professional counselors with individual patients and write a thesis on how my practice related to the major theories in the field. I was already quite accomplished in this field, so I was able to finish 63 credits of the program while also working full time as academic director of a college program and the Chair of the College Senate.

The BIG deal, from my point of view, however, was a three-credit project on "learning to control food." I had to read the nutrition literature, the dieting literature, the adult learning literature, and journal about how it informed by failure to attain and maintain my ideal weight. Then, I had to demonstrate my competency by implementing a program to succeed in losing my unhealthy and unwanted weight. This took seven years, but I worked on this project almost every day, and finally, I did it. Learning that perfectionism is one of the problems, I accepted an A- in the course for getting under 190 lbs. although I never got to 186 lbs.

I can still remember standing at graduation in my cap and gown. I had just designed and finished an innovative new graduate program, one of the most learner-centered and highest standard programs I knew about myself. It included ten bound book-length final papers and performance evaluations....but all I could think about was my flat stomach and that I had not been this weight since I was in high school. Also, that I was a little jittery – like I was on speed – as I had been on a previous diet. I had used a food plan popular in the 70's to get under 190. Just three months later, I had gained back 25 pounds. I experienced a level of demoralization that I never knew was possible.

I thought of starting to run again, but I could not get myself to do it. I thought of going back to the many academic resource people from my degree program and asking if they had any insights, but it seemed like it was too humiliating. I started reading books about death and dying; they were the only things that seemed to give me comfort. I also noticed that it was getting harder to do my work – work which I was passionate about and did at a level of mastery – at my current college. It was harder for me to deal with my colleagues, especially those to whom I reported. It was even hard to get into work in the morning. I would sit in the living room after my wife had gone to work and the kids went to school binging, watching TV or pornographic movies, knowing I would be an hour or two late to work. Then I would work too long and too late and almost fall asleep driving home. Many times, my eyes did close, and I swerved into the oncoming lane. It never occurred to me that this all was just the usual unmanageability of a late stage food and work addict.

Finally, it all came to a head. I created a somewhat dramatic confrontation with the administration of the college, and I was fired. I felt I was righteous in my cause at the time, but I now see it all as self-righteous manipulation. It took one more set of events to bring this home to me, at least initially. I used my organizing skills to get my job back. However, once the dust settled, I found myself almost uncontrollably starting fights – fights I did not want to have – with nearly everyone at work. I respectfully submitted my resignation.

Part Six

Back at home and without work, I started to look for employment. I was surprised to find that I was no longer seen as valuable for my experience initiating innovative college programs and I was ill-prepared and ill-suited for traditional college teaching or administration. I was seen as ill qualified for every position to which I applied. I started working at part-time positions on adjunct level wages. It was not enough money for our family to live on, but I did have a lot of extra time.

A chiropractor in my men's support group suggested a particular diet, "It's Not Your Fault You are Fat." I couldn't resist. The idea was that the diet would keep certain foods off my diet until a test meal. Over two months, there were a large number of food substances and categories of food tested. As I started this diet, I remember saying, "This is great! I can have as much as I want of the foods permitted each day. There is a wonderful variety from day to day. I could eat on this plan for the rest of my life." It didn't feel like a diet at all. I enjoyed it almost every day. On the nineteenth day, I had not had any sugar or wheat since I started, and lunch was the test meal for wheat. I was ecstatically looking forward to this meal. I baked a large loaf of whole wheat bread with nothing else but a little yeast. I planned to eat it all, and I also boiled up a large pot of spaghetti made just from wheat flour.

After several bites, I noticed a subtle feeling in my chest. It was hard to pay attention while I was eating, and I called for my then wife to come downstairs and help me pay attention to my experience. I kept eating as she made it downstairs. However, when she came into the kitchen, I stood up to greet her. My legs were unexpectedly weak; I fell to the floor. Almost immediately, I had the sense that I was going into shock. My whole body was weak, and I felt clammy and a little short of breath. I was feeling cold and shaking a little like I was afraid. From my previous training, I asked my wife to help me put my feet up on a chair and to cover me up with a blanket from the living room. I started worrying about going unconscious or into a coma. My wife asked if she should call 911. No, I responded. Instead, I asked her to keep talking to me. I had fainted or something, and I just needed to stay conscious. I told her about the test meal on wheat and kept reporting out what I was feeling. She had questions, and I did my best to answer them. It was quite a long time, ten or fifteen minutes, maybe twenty.

At one point, the reaction seemed to slow down. I tried to stand up and go into the next room, but it was too hard. So, I crawled on hands and knees into the living room and pulled myself up on the couch. "I'll be alright now," I said and decided to let myself fall off to sleep. I awoke a little later still a bit scared by the whole experience, but I was also very excited. "It was the food!" I kept saying to myself over and over. I was dramatically affected by the wheat and considering my long history of troubles around food and weight, it seemed like I might have finally stumbled onto the answer. "I just needed to stop eating wheat!" Again, it never occurred to me that I might not be able to do this.

Here is what I wrote much later about the next day. (It is long, but this is one of the most important experiences of my life, and the details turn out to be important, at least to me.):

I woke up with one clear goal—**not to eat any wheat**. *(I felt excited, calm and confident.)* **(It never occurred to me that I might not be able to do this.) (X—COMPLETE DENIAL OF POWERLESSNESS)** It seemed like a potentially a matter of life or death. *(I felt a little scared.)* **I was sure I could do it.** *(Self-reliant.)* I began as I often begin my weight loss diets, that is, by not eating any breakfast at all. *(I felt a little* *high, adrenalized.)* Instead, I got into some work around the house that I had been putting off for months. *(I felt "in the groove; productive.")*

Around 1pm, **I remembered I needed to eat** and made myself two baloney sandwiches with mayonnaise and mustard. (I felt a little anxious and anticipating eating.) **It didn't occur to me that the bread was made with wheat (X—MENTAL BLANK SPOT)** until I had taken several bites. (I felt surprised and scared.) Then I had a sinking feeling. **(X--POWERLESS) "Oh, this is exactly what I had decided not to do."** (I felt embarrassed, guilty and scared.) I quickly thought, **"I'm already eating wheat. I'll finish the sandwiches and start again tomorrow."** (I felt a little anxious, guilty, and relieved.)

The next day, I started out again with firm resolve. *(I felt committed, confident.)* **Again, it didn't occur to me that I might not be able to do this. (X—FORGETTING PAST CONSEQUENCES)** Again I skipped breakfast, and when lunch time rolled around, I made a large salad and threw on a tin of sardines. *(It was delicious.)* **I congratulated myself** after lunch for getting it right this time. *(I felt accomplished and less concerned.)* I also ate a healthy dinner of ground turkey, boiled red potatoes, and heated up a package of frozen green beans and carrots. *(I felt a little distracted and still a little hungry.)* I had a full second helping and was a bit stuffed when I spied an open package of Oreo cookies. **(X—PHYSICAL CRAVING TRIGGERED BY VISUAL IMAGE)** *(I lit up at the sight of the cookies.)* **"I haven't had dessert," I said to myself, so I decided I was entitled** to have one or two. *(I felt deserving.)* **(X--RATIONALIZATION) (I didn't consciously question or even notice that they contained wheat.) (X—MENTAL BLANK SPOT)** They were very good, so I had a couple more. **(X—PHYSICAL CRAVING)** *(I was eating them fast and compulsively.)* **I became** aware that these cookies were made of wheat flour and that I was not eating wheat for good reason, but my commitment to my health and my well being paled in contrast to my desire to eat Oreos. **(X—MENTAL OBSESSION)** I <u>wanted</u> the Oreos. **(X—PROGRESSIVE CRAVING)** Afterward, eating not just a couple but too many, *I felt guilty, consoled only by the thought that I could start again the next morning.* **(X—FALSE HOPE)**

The next morning, my choice to eat cookies the night before **seemed foolish**. *(I felt scared, guilty and embarrassed.)* I decided to eat breakfast this time and prepared a five-egg omelet with Colby cheese and leftover vegetables. I also poured myself a large glass of orange juice. *(I felt numb and satisfied; content.)* **(X—ADDICTIVE DENIAL)**

I went out for lunch with a friend, ordered a large bowl of chicken soup and some rice and beans. *(I felt a little excited.)* **Without even thinking,** I took a handful of little soda crackers from a bowl on the table and added them to my soup. **(X—PHYSICAL CRAVING TRIGGERED AGAIN)** *(I felt anticipatory.)* I had eaten several large spoonfuls of soup with soda crackers melting in before **I realized, "They're made from wheat**!" *I felt irritated with myself, embarrassed, and scared.* This was the third day I had broken my resolution to be wheat free. *(I felt disappointed.)* **"Oh, well, at least nothing happened—no queasy feeling in the chest and no fainting and falling on the floor."** **(X--MINIMIZATION)** *(I did feel concerned.)*

That night, I had a couple of turkey burgers, this time with rice and lots of butter. *(They tasted especially good.)* Instead of veggies, I had ice cream. *(It was delicious.)* **(I had no thought that I might have trouble with ice cream.)** **(X—LACK OF KNOWLEDGE; COMMON DENIAL)** After the second helping of ice cream, I picked up the ice cream carton and casually read the ingredients: "Milk, cream, sugar, wheat starch ... **wheat starch!"** *(I was surprised and started to blush.)* **I didn't know wheat was in so many foods. (X—LACK OF KNOWLEDGE; POWERLESS)** Moreover, I was getting really aggravated by my **"incompetence"** to follow my no wheat diet. *(Along with the anger, I started to feel ashamed.)* **(X—SHAME BASED ON FALSE ASSUMPTION ABOUT POWER)** I wrote myself a note and left it placed prominently on the kitchen table to help me remember ... **"No Wheat!"** the next day. **(X—BELIEF SLOGANS WILL WORK)** *(I felt worried but satisfied that I had done my best.)*

Day four. It was Sunday and planned as a day of rest. *(I felt calm and happy.)* I ate a couple of hard boiled eggs and an apple for breakfast. *(They tasted good, and I felt nourished.)* I saw the sign, "No Wheat!" **I thought about how often I used to make myself some cinnamon toast**

with this breakfast and very consciously patted myself on the back. (X—COMPLACENCY, DENIAL) *(I felt proud, even a little arrogant.)* Finally I was remembering to not eat wheat! *(I felt grateful and relieved.)* **(It didn't occur to me)**

Later that day, my ex-wife made Sunday dinner for the family (the kids were home from college) and one of her best friends. Before dinner, she offered to get drinks. It was the first time we had served alcohol to our kids. *(I felt a little concerned but confident and proud.)* I was pleased my wife was making drinks and had bourbon and soda. *(I wasn't all that interested in the drink but drank it anyway. I felt nonchalant.)* **It wasn't until the next day that it occurred to me that the liquor was made in part from grain. Wheat? (X—LACK OF KNOWLEDGE, POWERLESS)** *(I began to have a feeling of dread, but I didn't check it out.)*

On day five, **after realizing I had probably slipped again the night before,** I decided I might as well indulge and ate a whole sleeve of Fig Newtons through the afternoon and evening. **(X— EUPHORIC RECALL)** *(I was eating compulsively, hardly thinking about anything except getting the next cookie in my mouth.)* **(X—OUT-OF- CONTROL CRAVING)** Then my thinking changed; **I suddenly was committed again to not eating wheat.**

Finally, I told my ex-wife what was happening. *I was really disgusted with myself.* **(X—BASED ON FALSE NOTION OF MY OWN POWER)** I fessed up that I was so incompetent that I hadn't been able to do what I said for even one day. *(I suddenly had a much deeper realization about how wheat was at the core of my eating problem. I felt excited.)* Getting it all out, I felt better and **was determined** to start being wheat free on Tuesday. *(Telling it all to my ex-wife, I felt better and was now really determined to be wheat free the next day. I felt resolved and optimistic.)* **(X— BIOCHEMICAL DENIAL AGAIN)** It was like old times when I would start a **"new weight loss diet on Monday."** And that is how Tuesday started out.

I can't remember exactly when it started. In the morning, certainly by the sixth day, *I awoke with a dread.* **(X--POWERLESS)** The **memory of my "near death" experience when doing the test meal was** very vivid in my mind. It was still clear to me that wheat was potentially a very dangerous food substance for me. I needed to stop using it completely. *(I felt serious, concerned and determined.)* I had the thought, **"Maybe I wasn't having a strong reaction in several days because I didn't eat enough to trigger me."** (Later, **I speculated also that the reaction was not very strong because I was no longer detoxified**.) But I <u>was</u> having a reaction: I was eating wheat every day in spite of a strong commitment to abstain. **(X—SEEING THE TRUTH BUT NOT UNDERSTANDING IT) I didn't think of it that clearly yet,** but *I was deeply worried* when I caught myself eating wheat each day, more so as I kept being unable to stop as I thought I should be able to do like I used to do on diets or when giving up sweets for Lent. I might have had a slip every so often during Lent, but certainly not <u>every day</u>! **(X—PROGRESSIVE POWERLESSNESS)** *(I felt overwhelmed, disgusted with myself, scared.)*

So **I made up my mind again that morning to "give it my all."** *(I felt determined, strong, but a little uneasy.)* **(X--MINIMIZATION)** It was not just a good idea, reasonable and worth a try; it was **potentially life or death**. I had the thought, **"What if I get my legs knocked out from under me again, slipped into shock and then a coma? Was it possible that I might not come out of it?"** These thoughts may have been a little dramatic, that is, too extreme to be realistic; but at the time they felt very much within the realm of possibility, and *I was palpably scared.*

So **I committed to myself again that I would eat no wheat that day.** *(I felt determined, but not so confident.)* **(X--DEMORALIZED)** I planned out my meals ... eggs and rice cakes for breakfast, then a salad with lots of fresh greens and vegetables for lunch, plus a fruit ... steak, baked potato, cooked vegetables and a salad when I went out to dinner that evening with my wife. And that is what I ate. (I felt relieved, though still a little anxious and jittery.)

Driving home from the restaurant late, I opened up the glove compartment **for no reason, (X—MENTAL BLANK SPOT)** and there was a half-eaten graham cracker. *(I felt nothing.)* **(X)** I picked it up and shoved it in my mouth. **(X—NUMB; POWERLESS)** *(I felt* *compulsive.)* Realizing this was a wheat product, **I thought of spitting it out**, but instead chewed it well and swallowed it. **(X--CRAVING)** *(It was compulsive, and I felt crazy.)* **(X—IRRATIONAL THINKING) How could I do this again?** *(I felt hopeless.)*

I had the **image of myself flushing down a toilet bowl**. Neither my reason nor will power was of any help. I just kept eating wheat despite my very best intentions. **"I could die,"** I thought. *My heart sank,* and my next thought was, **"I am going to die, and there is nothing I can do about it." (X—LACK OF KNOWLEDGE, FALSE THINKING)** *(It was an awful sinking feeling.)* **"Sooner or later,** even just a little amount of wheat might take me down or drive me to eat more—and down the toilet I could go forever." That was my thinking, and I couldn't get it out of my head. *(I felt lost and in despair.)* **(X—SPIRITUAL EMPTINESS)**

The next morning, I awoke still preoccupied with my absolute inability to stop eating wheat. *(I felt complete despair.)* (X—SPIRITUAL BANKRUPTCY) I didn't even bother to make another commitment for the day. *(I felt it didn't matter.)* (X—SPIRITUAL POWERLESSNESS) I didn't eat any wheat at breakfast, lunch or dinner, but I thought, "Sooner or later I would ..." *(I felt hopeless and ashamed.)* (It never occurred to me that there might still be an answer.) (X—LACK OF KNOWLEDGE, POWERLESS)

That night I went to my men's support group meeting. *(I felt sad but convivial.)* As we started to talk, someone asked me how my diet was doing. I answered by telling the story of not being able to stop eating wheat for even a day, and I burst out crying. **(X—NO LONGER ABLE TO CONTAIN FEELINGS)** *(I sat there crying for a long time, 15 or 20 minutes or more.)* When I stopped, I got up and sat quietly. *(I felt still sad, but relieved.)* One of the other men said, "Can I give you some feedback?" *(I felt open.)* I nodded my head *yes*, and he went on, "You eat like I used to drink." That's all he said, but **it was immediately clear to me that he was an alcoholic, and I reacted to wheat just like an alcoholic relates to alcohol.** For the first time in my life, **I immediately recognized I was somehow addicted to wheat**. *(Oddly, this news was comforting. At least I was not somehow morally deficient or utterly incompetent as a human being.*

I had a disease, much like other people who were addicted to alcohol or drugs. There might even be a solution for me, too. I saw the glimmer of hope.)

Part Seven

It took me a while to find people who understood food addiction (they called it "compulsive overeating" at the time.) The first thing I heard was "Stop eating all of your binge foods and eat three moderate meal a day with nothing in between, one day at a time. I wrote down a lit of all the binge foods I could remember; there were 76. I thought, "life will not be worth living without all these foods, and I noticed that many contained wheat – which I now know I can't stop eating." However, in the context of being supported by other food addicts for whom this had worked, I went to any length the next day to eat abstinent of my specific binge foods as directed.

It was a very difficult day. I spent most of the day planning, shopping, preparing the three meals, eating, and cleaning up. It seemed like the tasks should not be very hard at all, but there was little time for anything else, and it was unexpectedly physically demanding to do this seemingly simple task. At the end of the day, though, I hadn't eaten any of my binge foods and, I was amazed, I hadn't eaten out of control at all. I was not convinced that this new way of abstinent eating would work, much less that I could do it again for even one more day. It seemed foolish not to try, however. So, I ate another day of moderate meals, nothing in between, without any of my binge foods. It still was not easy. Lots of difficult feelings came up. Since it worked, though, I kept doing it day after day. In fact, thirty years later, I have not eaten any of my binge foods, and I have not binged one day at a time. That is 10,957 back to back binge free days.

As a side benefit, I lost over 80 pounds in the first year and have maintained the same healthy weight – plus or minus three pounds – for twenty-nine years. Some other benefits: for the first time in my life, I actually have to throw out clothes that are the same size – not because I rubbed my pants thin between my thighs; I stopped ever having trouble climbing stairs, started fitting in airplane seats, and didn't break any more furniture just sitting down; my blood pressure and have stayed in a healthy range without medication; my hemorrhoids have stopped bleeding; my teeth seldom have cavities, and my gums have steadily healed; within two years, my compulsive thinking about food disappeared almost completely; after a few years, I started to slow down and was able for the first time to be able to meditate; I have been major depression free now (with the extra help of 40 mg of Prozac) for twenty years; though this may seem like no big deal to a normal eater, I am able to be rigorously honest about my food; and I have progressively developed a substantial spiritual life; I have regained my ability to work professionally and have a satisfying new career; I have much better relationships with my children, family and friends; I am – most of the time – happy, joyous and free.

There was a lot more work emotionally and spiritually to be able to maintain my weight loss and, more important, my food addiction recovery. I learned this from other food addicts who came before me, but that's another story. What has been the difference? I have treated myself as someone with a highly progressed disease of food addiction. By the grace of God and continued help of other food addicts, I hope to keep it up again today, and many more, one day at a time.

---

[1] This "incident of powerlessness (IOP) over food" was written by a protocol developed at the Glenbeigh Psychiatric Hospital of Tampa's residential food addiction program and later refined over twenty years as a way of challenging food addiction denial in five-day residential intensives. Basically, it starts out by the writing (or dictating) a description of what happened physically. Then, in layers, the feelings, thoughts, and "spiritual problem" are added. The IOP is read back to other food addicts in recovery for feedback. If more is remembered, this is added. In this document the descriptions are: the physical description in regular writing, feelings in italics, thinking bold faced, and the spiritual level of the experience in bold caps.

For some groups the conclusion of the reading and the accomplishment of weekly goals, SMARTEST ones, may be the ending of a successful experience with friends and with shared fulfillment. For others, this is a new beginning with the opportunity to continue the process identifying new weekly goals and sharing the celebrations and necessary changes.

For some individuals it may be the beginning of a new set of possibilities with increased support in group therapy, a 12-step recovery program, a support group related to your particular faith or belief system, or one-on-one therapy with an expert in the addiction(s) you have identified. Another alternative might be rehab for some who have found the withdrawals intolerable without medical support. In-house treatment sometimes means extended periods of time while for others it may be days to pass through the withdrawal. Whatever it is that you need to successfully accomplish your goals, please ask for what you need and be willing to accept those resources.

You've created a network here in this group and can continue to do so either in a continuation with these people or in another group.

You may find it helpful if you are disbanding, to have a check in date in a month to report on your steps to continue the process. Some groups do this monthly or quarterly for a year following the intense process you have shared. Discuss. Consider options that work for your members.

Best wishes as you reach out to request and receive what you need to succeed!

Please take time to report out on what changed and what you accomplished and how this process aided your efforts. Your shares will assist others on their paths. Please send pertinent material to: https://lightofcindy.wordpress.com/ and https://www.triggerfreenutrition.com

THEFIXforcravings@gmail.com and David@triggerfreenutrition.com

Remember Abstinence continues to be the best solution from triggers of all kinds.

Information on our gatherings, youtube, online presentations, and other opportunities for change are yours!

POSSIBLE FUTURE RESEARCH

If you have ideas about any of the items below, or if you have funding you wish to donate to accomplish some or all of the items below, please contact one of the authors!

1. Hormones: specifically, thyroid and what is "normal" at what ages and stages for individuals who experienced trauma and what interventions might ameliorate the differences from the norm of others?

2. Hormones: progesterone, estrogen, testosterone and what is "normal" at what ages and stages for individuals who have experienced trauma and what interventions might ameliorate the negatives?

3. Incidence rate of obesity, eating disorders, celiac disease in members of the Daughters and Sons of the American Revolution as they have birth, marriage, and death records of their ancestors back to the American Revolution in the 1770s and 80s. (For those who agree with the posited epigenetic changes due to starvation in the time of the pregnancy prior to the birth of an infant, this research might facilitate the genetic changes in the United States in 340 years.)

4. A meta-analysis of the effects on self-regulation systems when people engage in yoga, tango, tai chi, kickboxing, martial arts, choral singing, (Elementary: the stick and rubber figure capasawra), boxing, mindfulness, meditation, chanting, Jazzercise…

5. Consideration of diagonal slippage through generations: aunt to niece rather than mother to daughter and the concomitant relational and genetic predispositions with potential interventions

6. Change systems and which are those components of individual choice and those impacted by codependency/relational elements involving others: how to intervene with positive relational strategies to support individual choice

7. Comorbidity and clustering predispositions for disorders, diseases, and conditions may be another area in which additional research could aid those with obesity and other addictions. Alcoholism, drug addiction, sex addiction, nicotine addiction, sugar addiction, fat addiction, grain addiction, cluttering, migraines, "too many intestines," sexual abuse, cutting, self-harming with work addiction and other instruments of pain and pleasure, under-earning, risk taking, multiple marriages and divorces, debting, acquiring more degrees and/or credentials than one reasonably needs, love addiction, and the list goes on. (Those are on my own personal list. You may have others.)

8. Cultural factors

9. Ethnic factors

10. Genetic factors (I am curious about my Jewish genes and the incidence of sugar and grain addiction amongst people like me.)

11. Economic factors including both poverty and wealth

12. Spiritual solutions including twelve-step programs and for whom do they work/not work?

13. Suicidal ideation and suicide attempts: desperation and what is its part?

14. How does abstinence from specific substances and/or behaviors support freedom from cravings (physical first and then emotional, mental, and spiritual?)

15. How much support and of what varieties offer the most success to those seeking freedom from the phenomenon of craving?

16. "I want to be normal" has what meaning and what potential benefits or liabilities for those who have differences in their bodily, mental, emotional, and/or spiritual make up?

17. What is normal? Does the DSM-V purport to define the norm when it excluded food addiction?

18. What is the role of trauma in eating disorders (anorexia, bulimia, binge eating disorder) as compared with food addiction?

19. How might eating disorders be treated differently than food addiction to gain increased success for all.

20. Might the hormonal changes related to child abuse be correlated with endometriosis and dysmenorrhea and LLPDD ? How might these be ameliorated?

21. Might oxytocin (too much or too little) be instrumental in creating or ameliorating effects of trauma?

22. Might testosterone (too much or too little) be instrumental in creating or ameliorating effects of trauma?

23. Is food addiction another autoimmune disease?

24. What effect does the gut biome have in relation to food addiction. What strategies can change the gut biome?

APPENDIX A

A QUESTIONNAIRE for you to share, if you wish by sending to THEFIXforcravings@gmail.com

If you want to be part of a data collection project to potentially help others, please complete the questionnaire in the appendices and send your results to us.

A questionnaire for each reader to consider for his or her own awareness and potentially to share with the authors for a future collaborative resource for others:

Which of these have I experienced?

Which of these has a parent experienced?

Which of these has a grandparent experienced?

Which has a sibling experienced?

Which of these has an offspring experienced?

At what age? For each person?

Listing of concomitant difficulties

	Self	Parent	Grandparent	Sibling	Offspring
Anorexia					
Bulimia					
Disordered Eating					
Eating Addiction					
Food Addiction					

	Self	Parent	Grandparent	Sibling	Offspring
List of specific foods with allergic responses					
Allergies to foods					
List of specific "problem" foods					
Manic Depression					
Mood Swings					
Bipolar Disease					
Panic					
Dysthymia					
Late Luteal Phase Dysphoric Disorder					
Premenstrual Syndrome					
Heart Palpitations					
Migraines					
Headaches					
Visual Disturbances					
Hormone Irregularities "Birth Pains" at Periods Excessive Bleeding Clotting Mood Swings					
Weight Gain					
Yoyo weight gain and loss					
Weight Loss					
Participation in diets, list as many as you recall with the outcome for each					
Participation in Food Rehab Program(s), list time frame and outcome, list the name of program, place					
Abstinence, when and Time lengths from what substances or behaviors					
Anxiety					

	Self	Parent	Grandparent	Sibling	Offspring
Fear					
Isolation					
Extraversion					
Introversion					
Lap Band Surgery					
Bariatric Surgery or other					
Therapy					
Chiropractic Care					
Massage Therapy					
Colonic Therapy					
Appendicitis					
Ovarian Cysts					
Cystic Breasts					
Smoking					
Quitting Smoking					
# Years Free from Smoking					
Pot Smoking					
# Years Free from Smoking Pot					
Trauma Number(s) _____ Please see list on p ...					
# Years Free From					

APPENDIX B

The Smartest Goals

Smart goals are available on the Internet with numerous explanations. Smarter goals, likewise. Smartest goals:

S Specific:
   Who?
   What?
   When?
   Where?
   And why?
   These questions if answered will provide the best goals

M – Measurable:

   How will you be able to know if you have succeeded or not?
   How many times?
   How much?
   How many?
   Be specific.

A – Agreed:

   With whom do you need agreements?
   Family?
   Close friends?
   A support group or groups?
   Oneself?
   A spiritual commitment or covenant?

R - Realistic:

Achievable and demanding but not impossible within the time frame (next step.)

T - Time Defined:

You commit to complete this goal by when?
Be specific as this confines the unending possibilities!
Different goals may have different time frames allowed for completion.
Making "Swiss Cheese commitments" (i.e., smaller holes in a larger goal) make accomplishments more accessible.

E - Ethical: Living with your highest ethical standards supports success. This is quite individual; however, your collaborative intention to support your of their goal.

S - Succinctly Recorded: The goal written down in brief sentences makes it available for review, evaluation, and celebration when completed.

T - Thought Out Carefully: We often achieve our goals and then find there were missing pieces. Be attentive to what you seek for you may be successful! (At one time my husband and I were seeking homeownership near the Pacific or the Atlantic Oceans; however, we frequently talked about it as living near "water." When we found our new condo, it was overlooking Lake Michigan, which is water and appears to be an ocean! Were we successful?)

RECIPES DO YOU HAVE ONES TO SHARE WHICH ARE YOURS TO GIVE? (NO GRAIN, SUGAR, OR ALCOHOL PLEASE.)

APPENDIX C

Sugars List

Common Names of Sugars and Sweeteners

Oses:

Dextrose 1
Fructose (any type)
Galactose
Glucose
Lactose
Levulose
Maltodextrose
Maltose
Polydextrose
Ribose
Sucrose
Xyulose

Sugar:

Barbados sugar
Beet sugar
Cane sugar
Confectioners' sugar
Dark brown sugar
Date sugar
Donut Sugar
Fruit sugar
Granulated sugar
Grape sugar
Invert sugar
Light brown sugar
Lite sugar
Maple sugar (any type)
Powdered sugar
Raw sugar
Sugar (any type)
Turbinado sugar
White sugar

Molasses:

Molasses (any kind)

Cane:

Cane Juice (any type)
Crystallized cane juice (any type)
Dehydrated cane juice (any type)
Florida crystals™
Raw cane crystals

Malt:

Barley extract
Malt
Malt flavoring
Malted barley
Malted cereal extract
Rice malt

Fruit:

Clarified grape juice
Fruit juice concentrate
Fruit juice sweeteners
Fruit nectars
Fruitsource™
Monk fruit extract

Sugar Alcohol:

Erythritol
Malitol
Mannitol
Sorbitol
Xylitol

Syrup:

Agave syrup
Brown rice syrup
Cane syrup
Fruit syrup
High fructose corn syrup
Hydrogenated glucose syrup
Invert sugar syrup
Invert syrup
Malt syrup
Maple syrup
Natural syrup
Ribbon cane syrup
Rice syrup
Sorghum syrup
Malt syrup
Corn syrup

Sweeteners:

Brown rice sweetener
Corn sweeteners
Corn syrup solids
Fruit sweetener
Saccharine
Stevia
Sucralose

Dextrin:

Dextrin
Lactodextrin tapioca
Lactylated dextrin
Maltodextrin
Honey:
Honey (any kind)

Adapted from Sugars with Permission by H. Theresa Wright MS, RD, LDN copyright 1994, 1996, 2006 Renaissance Nutrition Center Inc.

BIBLIOGRAPHY

Avena, N. (2017). *The Challenges Posed By the Modern Food Environment and How They Relate to Addictive Overeating.* The Food Addiction Institute.

Banks, S., & Dinges, D. (2007). Behavioral and Physiological Consequences of Sleep Restriction, *3*, 519-528.

Brown, H.J. (2012). *Life's Little Instruction Book.* Thomas Nelson Inc.

Davis, J. M., Zhao, Z., Stock, H. S., Mehl, K. A., Buggy, J., & Hand, G. A. (2003). Central nervous system effects of caffeine and adenosine on fatigue, *284*(2), R399-R404. https://doi.org/10.1152/ajpregu.00386.2002

Davis, W. (2014). *Wheat Belly* (pp. 124-125). New York: Rodale Books.

El-Sharkawy, A. M., Sahota, O., & Lobo, D. N. (2015). Acute and chronic effects of hydration status on health, *73*(suppl 2), 97-109. https://doi.org/10.1093/nutrit/nuv038

Holick, M. F. (2004). Sunlight and vitamin D for bone health and prevention of autoimmune diseases, cancers, and cardiovascular disease, *80*(6), 1678S-1688S. https://doi.org/10.1093/ajcn/80.6.1678s

Kris-Etherton, P. M., Grieger, J. A., & Etherton, T. D. (2009). Dietary reference intakes for DHA and EPA, *81*(2-3), 99-104. https://doi.org/10.1016/j.plefa.2009.05.011

Lustig, R. H. (2012). *Fat Chance* (p. 69). Penguin.

Mori, T. A. (2014). Dietary n-3 PUFA and CVD: a review of the evidence, *73*(01), 57-64. https://doi.org/10.1017/s0029665113003583

Perlmutter, D. (2013). *Grain Brain* (pp. 70-71). New York: Little, Brown.

Pludowski, P., Holick, M. F., Pilz, S., Wagner, C. L., Hollis, B. W., Grant, W. B., Shoenfeld, Y., Lerchbaum, E., Llewellyn, D. J., & Kienreich, K. (2013). Vitamin D effects on musculoskeletal health, immunity, autoimmunity, cardiovascular disease, cancer, fertility, pregnancy, dementia and mortality—A review of recent evidence, *12*(10), 976-989. https://doi.org/10.1016/j.autrev.2013.02.004

Tarman, V. (2014). *Food Junkies*. Dundurn.

Medium.com/@nilsparker/the angel-in-the-marble-f7aa43f333dc

Armstrongmcguire.com/blog/defining-time-talent-and-treasure January 19,2017 by Leslie Starsoneck

Challenging Food Addiction Denial – physically, emotionally, mentally and spiritually by Phil Werdell in the ACORN Primary Intensive Handbook.

Printed in the United States
By Bookmasters